A Century of Service

DIRECTORS

Pearl
Mitchell
1918-1924

Rev. Emory
Barnes
1926-1934

Edward N.
Powell
1934-1945

Lee Roy
Pettiford
1947-1962

John
Caldwell
1962-1964

Reginald
Gary
1964-1965

James
Horn
1965-1968

Moses L.
Walker
1968-1978

Gordon
Brown
1978-1980

Nathaniel
McCaslin
1981

Rick C.
Frazier
1981-1986

Rev. Guyron
Philbert
1987

Michael
Williams
1987-2006

(Interim)
Valerie
Cunningham
2006

Tim
Terrentine
2006-2010

(Interim)
James
Greene
2011-2013

Sherry
Thomas-Cloud
2013-2016

Cheree L.
Thomas
2016-2018

Sidney
Ellis
2018---

No Photo
Mr. Miller
1924 -1926

Edward Lewis
1945

John Ridley
1946 -1947

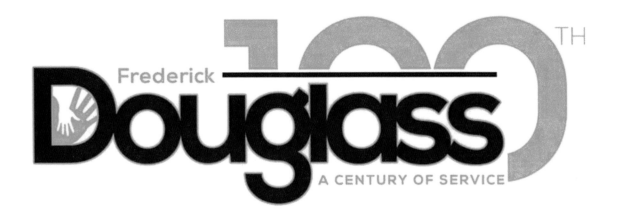

A Century of Service

Copyright 2020

SEASON Press LLC

Kalamazoo, Michigan

Douglass Community Association
1000 West Paterson Street • Kalamazoo, Michigan 49007
https://www.dcakalamazoo.com

Ordering Information:
Special discounts are available on quantity purchases by corporations, associations, and for
U.S. trade bookstores and wholesalers. For details, contact the publisher.

Book design by Sean Hollins, Fortitude Graphic Design and Printing
Author/Historian Sonya Hollins
Consultant Editor, Margaret Zahrai
Published in collaboration with Season Press, LLC

Library of Congress Control Number: 2020908278
A Century of Service: 100 Years of the Douglass Community Association

1. Douglass Community Association —History —Michigan History 2. Recreation Associations —
United States 3. African American— History 4.Frederick Douglass 5. Kalamazoo, Michigan

ISBN Paperback: 978-1-7328399-6-0
ISBN Hardbound: 978-1-7328399-9-1

First Edition
10 9 8 7 6 5 4 3 2 1

Printed in the United States of America

*Dedicated to Forrest Hill
whose compassion for Colored soldiers
forever changed a community.*

Table of Contents

A Big Band performance and religious play were examples of the cultural
activities held at the Douglass Community Center from its inception.
(Douglass Community Association Archives)

FOREWORD

Speak Life: What the Douglass Community Association Did for Me

I was raised on Kalamazoo's north side where the community grocery store was in walking distance. As a preteen, my friends and I often strolled along Paterson Street to the neighborhood Family Foods grocery store on Douglas Avenue. It was during that time in the early 80s that I noticed a big sign in a grassy field across from the store that read:

FUTURE HOME OF THE DOUGLASS COMMUNITY ASSOCIATION

Many of our lives changed once the Douglass was completed. We had a place to play where people cared about us and our futures. As I reflect on how the volunteers of the Douglass were there to guide and shape my life, seed planters like Gus Calbert and Wally Olson were instrumental.

Coach Calbert spoke life into me and helped me understand the consequences of my decisions. Olson was the father of Jeff, one of my lifelong friends and Douglass basketball teammates. As a successful businessman, he sponsored our entire team on a trip to attend a championship game in Stockholm, Sweden. This led me to dream of world travel. As a result, I ended up doing just that. I have traveled the world as a senior executive to lead employees in countries such as China, Brazil, India, Singapore, Japan, and England.

My biological and Douglass family spoke life into me. Now, as an adult and successful businessman and author, I have the ability to sow seeds into others and pay it forward. In this book, those such as director Lee Roy Pettiford, Moses Walker, and Michael Williams led the charge for youth and community mental health. Staff members like John Caldwell and Juanita Goodwin set the tone for what true dedication to the lives of young people looked like. All of us have that ability. For 100 years, the staff and volunteers of the Center planted seeds into the lives of thousands, young and old, and of diverse backgrounds.

This book shares the story of an organization that changed me...and a community. The decades of impact on the community can fill volumes, and this first-ever history of the organization celebrates the legacy. The Douglass changed my life. I pray this book will inspire and motivate the readers to cherish and continue the story for the next 100 years and beyond.

Fenorris Pearson is a native of Kalamazoo who attended Eastern Michigan University on a full basketball scholarship, thanks to the Douglass Community Association. He has worked for Dell and Motorola, is an Amazon bestselling author, and is a philanthropist who pays it forward by providing Dell computers, scholarships, and paid internships to youth from his community. Parts of his tribute to the Douglass during its 100th anniversary were used for this foreword.

Introduction
A Community Legacy

There is no way to sum up the magnitude of such a celebration as this. The Frederick Douglass Community Association, or "the Douglass" as it is affectionately referred to, has developed based on the needs of the community at different moments in time. Many do not know that the Douglass was originally established to meet the social needs of Black soldiers stationed at Camp Custer (now Fort Custer) in Battle Creek, Michigan, during World War I. During our 2019 Community Family Cookout one of the attendees pointed out that, because of Douglass' close association with Black soldiers, one of the soldiers met her mother (a local Kalamazoo woman). The two married—thus her family was established. How many others have that type of testimony?

As the needs of the community have changed, so has the focus of the Douglass. Those who come through the doors to inspire others include educators, professionals, Scout leaders, athletes, outdoorsmen, and those in the arts. These are examples of the positive influences so many people of all ages have experienced at the Douglass. We have consistently helped to develop the lives of our community members even when our locations changed. We moved from the upper floor of the Turn Verein Hall on North Burdick Street, to our first-owned building on Ransom Street, and finally, to our current building on Paterson Street. Although we are known as the hub of the Northside community of Kalamazoo, the Douglass always has been a safe, loving environment for all.

The theme of the 100th Year Celebration was "Shaking the Hand of the Past and Welcoming the Hand of the Future." More than five thousand people came through the doors of the Douglass each month during the summer of 2019. They took part in such programs as summer camp, the "Meet Up and Eat Up" community lunch program, food giveaways (warm meals and produce), employment skill building, music lessons, free diapers, library resources, and a host of other services. And today's needs are much different than yesterday's.

Today, our kids begin to use computer devices and phones as early as their young hands can hold them. So we must keep up with the times by providing students access to the same type of technology they use in school to do their homework. As society's needs change, we plan to continue to adjust to accommodate those requirements.

For the past 100 years, diverse partners have helped us fulfill our mission to create a culture of equity and inclusion that transforms the lives of Northside residents and others throughout the city. Through effective, efficient, and quality opportunities offered through the Douglass, we will continue to be a vital part of the community for years to come.

Remarks by Executive Director Sidney A. Ellis during the 100th Anniversary gala of the Frederick Douglass Community Association on September 28, 2019, at Western Michigan University.

The Douglass Community Center located
at 231 E. Ransom St. around 1950s.
(Kalamazoo Public Library)

S. Burdick, North Kalamazoo, Mich · K.2

South Burdick Street around late 1800s.
(Kalamazoo Valley Museum)

> "Well, we need help. Tell you what. Joe, you go to some of them gentlemen at the City Hall. Otis, you talk to Eddie Desenberg. Joe, Mr. Gilmore or (Mr.) Light, or even Upjohns might listen to you."
>
> Forrest Hill

Right: Michigan Traction Company interurban rails transported soldiers from Camp Custer to Kalamazoo. (Kalamazoo Valley Museum)

"That's why we've got to do something."

The Beginning

1919

Community members dance at first
Frederick Douglass Community
Center, 228 N. Burdick Street circa 1920s.
(Douglass Community Association)

It was in the war, and the young women often went there for dances, or to help the soldiers write letters home. The soldiers came from Battle Creek on the "interurban" which was like a trolley that ran to Battle Creek and Gull Lake.

Dolly Brown Davis recalls the original Frederick Douglass Community Center. "They Helped Fight Loneliness," *Kalamazoo Gazette*, September 25, 1987.

After hundreds of years of slavery in America, the anticipated quest for freedom came with devastating emotional trauma for African Americans—freed or enslaved. The Emancipation Proclamation document signed by President Abraham Lincoln on January 1, 1863, declared all slaves free. However, the Civil War between the North and the South continued until April 9, 1865. The War exposed stark divisions between North and South, Confederate and Union, free and slave states. But regardless of which side a soldier fought, the ability to accept those with any percentage of African blood as humans deserving of a right to live a life free of racism would not come easy.

Forrest M. Hill did not grow up on a plantation in the South. He claimed that his family had never been enslaved and had worked hard with their own hands to provide for themselves. Hill was born on October 11, 1852, in Cass County, Michigan. The farmer eventually married Flora on February 15, 1872, and they moved to Kalamazoo with their children. Despite the resistance from White farmers, Hill was encouraged by a White landowner who sold him land for a farm on the outskirts of the city, now known as West Main.

He came to Kalamazoo to work not in a servant role, but as an entrepreneur. His skills as a laborer and the benefit of possessing his own tools and horse team allowed him to secure work as an independent contractor on buildings and roads. His huge sturdy build and proud demeanor commanded respect. While he understood the bold objections and ostracism he and his family received from White neighbors, he would not tolerate any threats of physical attacks on anyone, particularly his granddaughter, Pauline, who they affectionately called Polly.

Mr. Hill with Pauline 1920

Above: Pauline Byrd Johnson poses with Grandpa Forrest Hill in 1920s. Right: Forrest and wife, Flora married in 1872. (*Kalamazoo News*)

Mr & Mrs. Forrest Hill

When Polly came home from Vine Street School and told of how one White boy pulled her hair and called her derogatory names with no intervention from teachers, Grandpa Hill took matters into his own hands. He rode his horse and wagon up to the front door of the home that belonged to the

Pauline Johnson

boy's prominent family. He introduced himself, explained the situation, and gave the father a choice. Either the father would correct the son or Grandpa Hill would. That boy never picked on Polly again. And while children and teachers continued to call her names and attempt to make her feel dirty and ignorant despite her intelligence, Grandpa Hill taught her to always carry herself with respect and not lower herself to the ways of others.

Above: Pauline Byrd Johnson. (Kalamazoo College)
Right: Vine Street School circa 1910. (Kalamazoo Public Library)

Grandpa Hill and his wife Flora were dedicated members of Allen Chapel A.M.E. Church, one of the first Colored churches in the city. He was respected by prominent White men in the community who stood up for him when he wanted to purchase land. Others helped him secure contracts to work on projects such as Kalamazoo College. His home on Parker Street (now Pioneer Street) was often a meeting place for men to talk about community and church business. One evening, Polly sat in the kitchen while Grandpa Hill and his friends discussed Colored soldiers.

Inset image: Simpson M.E. Church (currently site of Allen Chapel A.M.E., 1909. (Kalamazoo Public Library)

U. S. AT WAR: WILSON

U-BOAT SINKS AZTEC, ARMED U. S. STEAMER

Americans in Crew Are Believed Victims of Blow in Dark.

NOW FOR THE DE

WARNINGS TO GERMAN

BOTH HOUSE HASTEN W ON

"WE MUST FIGHT JUSTICE AND

President Tells Joint Sess That German Mea to All

Above: Chicago Daily Tribune headlines war April 6, 1917.
The famous African American regiment, Harlem
Hellfighters, arrives from France, 1919.
(National Archives-Records of War Department-Group 165)

The 1914 assassination of the Austrian Archduke Franz Ferdinand and his wife triggered deadly fighting involving Austria, Serbia, Germany, Russia, France, Britain, Japan, Turkey, Italy, and Romania. The United States attempted to remain neutral in the war across the Atlantic. However, the tide turned when Germany used its submarines to sink Allied, neutral, and U.S. ships in the British Isles. America could no longer idly stand by. On April 6, 1917, President Woodrow Wilson declared war on Germany.

That call to arms unleashed $250 million in federal funds to assist with war efforts, including the training of additional troops. Battle Creek Michigan's Chamber of Commerce agreed to begin construction of a new 16,000-acre training base on July 1, 1917. It would be named in honor of Civil War General George A. Custer. In less than two months, nearly 100,000 troops from across the country arrived to train at Camp Custer, and Colored soldiers of the 536th Engineer Service Battalion were among them.

The surge of soldiers on Battle Creek led to a need for off-duty places to relax between training and active duty in Europe. In 1900, the electric Interurban Rail between Kalamazoo and Battle Creek was created. This electric rail became a popular mode of transportation for thousands of soldiers who ventured from Battle Creek on the rail that ran through Augusta, Gull Lake, and Kalamazoo.

Right: Memorabilia from the days of the Interurban Rail. (Kalamazoo Valley Museum)
Below: Camp Custer during World War II. (Library of Congress)

Camp Custer, Battle Creek, Michigan

L. N. DOWNS, President & Gen'l Mgr.

DEE ALLEN, Vice Pres. & Secretary   C. C. BEACH, Treas.

W. D. HAWLEY, Supt.   F. O. GRISWOLD, Supt.
Kalamazoo Division   Battle Creek Division

Michigan Traction Co.,

KALAMAZOO, MICH.

Interurban Line runs between BATTLE CREEK
and KALAMAZOO and passes GULL LAKE.

25

COMPLETE VIEW OF CAMP CUSTER, MICH.
JULY 1918.

Forrest Hill: "Men, we've got to do something. Things can't go on like this. Hanging around on street corners is going to get these boys in trouble with the police."

Joe Pettiford: "Brother Hill's right. There's nothing some of these officers would like better than to run in some of our boys."

Otis Pratt: "Sure would. You know they think we shouldn't be soldiers, anyway."

Other men like Joe Small and Joseph Pettiford: "That's why we've got to do something. We've got to show them that we are men, same as anyone else. We've got to take care of our own."

Forrest Hill: "Well, we need help. Tell you what, Joe, you go to some of them gentlemen at the City Hall. Otis, you talk to Eddie Desenberg. Joe, Mr. Gilmore or Mr. Light, or even Mr. Upjohn might listen to you. I know some men at Bryant (Paper Mill) or Nazareth and some other places who I can approach. Let's tell them our trouble and see what we can do."

Much of the narrative for this chapter came from the article, "The Beginning," by Pauline Johnson, published in the Souvenir Program booklet in 1984 to celebrate the opening of the new 1000 W. Paterson St. Douglass Community Association.

A few evenings later...

Otis Pratt worked for Eddie Desenberg, a local philanthropist and grocer. Desenberg had purchased land in Mattawan in 1916 as a summer camp for the inner-city youth of all races. His desire was to take children out of the city and provide them with healthy meals and fresh air during the summer at a place called Pretty Lake Camp. Pratt shared the concern for the Colored soldiers with Desenberg, who then arranged a meeting with the local branch of the National Recreation Association under the leadership of R.O. Brundage.

Brundage created the War Camp Community Service and solicited guidance and support from local philanthropists that Forrest and his friends knew and admired, such as John Ryan, Stanley Morris, Fred M. Hodge, and pharmaceutical leader Harold Upjohn. They all realized potential issues when the more than "4,000 Colored soldiers sometimes poured into Kalamazoo within a few hours," (*Kalamazoo Gazette*, June 2, 1935).

The first order of business would be to find a place where Colored soldiers could come and have organized programming and activities. Turn Verein Hall, located in the 200 block of North Burdick, was originally created in a true German gymnasium style. The three-story Turn Verein, used as a meeting place by various organizations in the community since 1881, suddenly became available. The third floor was put to use as a gathering place for Colored soldiers. Funds were raised to pay for the rent, furniture, food, and other amenities.

Excitement grew among White and Colored citizens to create a place of prestige and social vigor. The place would now need a name specifically for their purpose. Many names were suggested, including names of prominent and respected leaders of Kalamazoo. However, Forrest Hill had another idea. While he may not have realized it at the time, his suggested namesake was symbolic to the soldiers this new place would serve.

Michigan Avenue and Burdick Street around 1920s.
(Kalamazoo Public Library Local History Room Photograph File P-1060)

Frederick Douglass was born in 1818 and eventually escaped from slavery. He spoke boldly against slavery, founded his own newspaper, the North Star, and was a proponent of Colored men serving in the Union Army. He changed his name from Frederick Augustus Washington Bailey to Frederick Douglass and lived the rest of his life in the Washington, D.C., area. He penned his memoirs, was appointed U.S. Minister to Haiti, served as a presidential elector, and was appointed U.S. Marshal for the District of Columbia.

After the Civil War, Douglass continued to lecture. According to articles in the Enquirer and News (Sunday, November 8, 1959), Douglass was in Battle Creek on various occasions from Emancipation Day celebrations to lectures sponsored by the Battle Creek Literary Association. During a three-day lecture series there in 1884, he spoke on "Self-Made Men," "The Unity of the Races," and "The Designs of Slave Power," and earned $300 for those presentations. He stayed in the home of prominent African American barber John J. Evans, who owned the largest barbershop in Battle Creek, mostly serving a White clientele.

Smithsonian National Museum of African American History and Culture.

Douglass died on February 20, 1895, at the age of 78. Douglass' home is now part of the National Park Services and his name graces schools, neighborhoods, and parks throughout the country. While Forrest Hill may not have ever attended an event to hear Douglass speak, he admired what he read about the abolitionist as a fearless leader who was revered by Colored and Whites alike. What better namesake for a center for Colored soldiers than Frederick Douglass?

"Once let the black man get upon his person the brass letters 'U.S.,' let him get an eagle on his button and a musket on his shoulder and bullets in his pockets and there is no power on earth which can deny that he has earned the right to citizenship in the United States."
Frederick Douglass

First Skyscraper, Under Construction, Kalamazoo, Mich.

Kalamazoo National Bank, 1909. (Kalamazoo Valley Museum)

"Our Negro soldiers had a place to get together for rest or fun or food at a place all our own named Frederick Douglass Center."

Pauline Johnson

Right: Soldiers and community members relax at the first Douglass Community Center. (Douglass Community Association Archives)

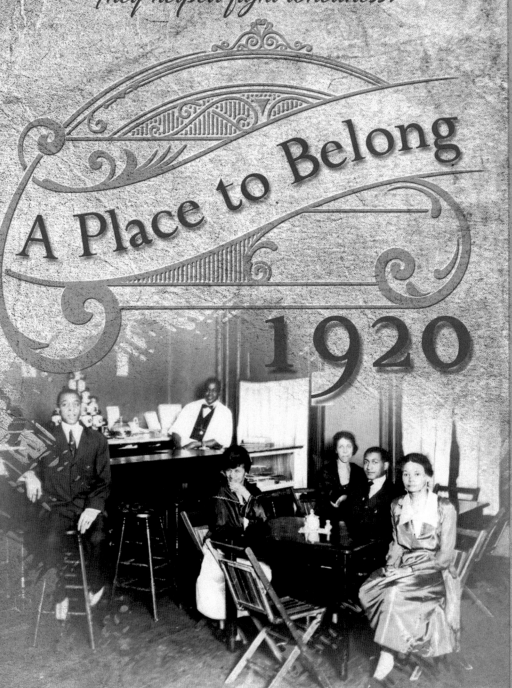

"They helped fight loneliness."

A Place to Belong

1920

"The Douglass Community Center stands as both Y.M.C.A. and Y.W.C.A for the colored boy and girl; rendering to them the assistance that self-respect and good citizenship demand."

Community Chest (now United Way) annual grantee description, 1928.

The Y.M.C.A. circa 1913, downtown Kalamazoo. (Kalamazoo Public Library)

Prior to World War I and the resulting need to provide a place for Colored soldiers to socialize, Kalamazoo's ethnically-diverse community included German-born residents who had immigrated to America. One area in downtown Kalamazoo included so many German-owned businesses that it was known as the German Business District. These new citizens brought the best of German culture and opened businesses that accentuated everything from food to clothing. Proprietors owned such places as Rosenbaum Factory, Reck's Watches and Jewelry, H. Roediger's Furniture Store, Prange Building, Columbus Saloon, George Hanselman's Candy Factory, Hepp's Clothing, and Maus Drugstore.

What most impressed Americans was the introduction to German exercise facilities called Turn Vereins. These gymnasium-type facilities provided a place where firemen and others who wanted to stay fit could do so through the use of horizontal bars, trapeze, rings, the pommel horse, and other equipment. An article in the *Kalamazoo Daily Telegraph* noted the opening of a new building that may have had one of the finest Turn Vereins and provided, "One of the most convenient and comfortable halls in the State...it is a credit to Kalamazoo," (March 22, 1881).

In the book, *Yes, There Were Germans in Kalamazoo* (Kalamazoo Historical Society, 1979) author Elizabeth Mayer described the immaculate three-story (Turn Verein) Hall located at 226 North Burdick Street (the street numbers changed over the years and it became 228 by 1919). The Hall contained a parlor, dining room, kitchen, smoking and cloakrooms, a stage for music performances, reception rooms, apartments, and its famed gymnastic area. By the end of its first year, nearly fifty Americans had secured memberships at the Hall to take part in the social and physical activities.

However, the love affair with the Hall and its founders began to fade shortly after the turn of the century. It was then, in 1914, that conflict and war in Europe made worldwide news. When the United States declared war on Germany, local Germans who had roots in their new home now felt the tension. Some began to lose favor in their once beloved community and the Turn Verein era was over.

The enormous Dutch influence in here, coupled with World War I, tended to obscure the German immigrant contribution to Kalamazoo. While little German involvement here before 1860 has been documented, it is known that tens of thousands of Germans headed toward Michigan around 1860 as a result of the state's promotional efforts.

American agents in Germany recruited from all over the nation and some of the immigrants ended up in Kalamazoo.

The Germans were mostly city folks, businessmen and shopkeepers who preferred to remain downtown. They owned and managed hotels, groceries, restaurants, shoe stores, clothing shops and other retail businesses.

KALAMAZOO
"GERMAN BUSINESS DISTRICT"

KEY TO BUILDINGS

1. Folz Building at "Folz Corner"; after 1892. (1874 Peninsular Building of Nicholas Baumann.)
2. Hepp's Clothing Store. (Formerly Weber's Boots and Shoes; since 1880's. Also Fischer's Meat Market.)
3. Mittenthal Bros. (1899.)
4. Mary Kriechbaum. (1908.)
5. Button and Jannasch. (Marked 1869.)
6. William E. Kreeger. (Marked 1924.)
7. Jannasch-Shortt Musical Institute. (1878-1909.)
8. Schau Building. (ca 1900.)
9. Rosenbaum Building.
10. Maus Drugstore. (After 1897.)
11. Rosenbaum Factory.
12. Columbia Hotel of Adam Ehrmann; after 1897. (Home of Emil Friedmann in that area in 1880's.)
13. George Hanselman's early candy factory. (After 1880.)
14. Columbus Saloon; in German hands.
15. Star Paper Company of Selig Stern.
16. American Hotel of Fred Hotop. (After 1869.)
17. Everard and Ihling; since 1870's.
18. Desenberg Wholesale Grocery. (Designed in 1885.)
19. Meyer Cramer Clothing. (1880.)
20. Berghoff Hotel and Cafe. (After 1910. Witwer, Bakery; Adolf Seiler, Restaurant; G. Philipp, Saloon; Moritz Lenz, Dyer; Scherer Bros., Barbers; Leopold Hofer, Shoemaker, located in that area in 1880's.)
21. Germania Hotel.
22. Louis Ehrmann Hotel. (Erected in 1904.)
23. Western Hotel of Adam Ehrmann.
24. Louis Ehrmann Saloon.
25. Rickman Hotel. (Owned by Leo Ehrman 1925-1950.)
26. Ehrmann Saloon
27. Turn Verein Hall (Since 1880.)
28. A Baumann Block. (Constructed in 1881.)
29. Engelmann Saloon. (The old Engelmann farm was in this area on Water Street.)
30. Fuerst Stables.
31. H. and L. Stern Clothing. (After 1870's.)
32. Hanselman Building. (1913-1973.)
33. Fred Limprecht's German Saloon in Fireman's Hall. (Around 1860.)
34. Reck's Watches and Jewelry. (Still in 1970.)
35. A.U.V. "Auditorium". (Built in 1898. "Arbeiter Hall" on same site since 1873.)
36. H. Roediger's Furniture Store; Carl C. Meisterheim, Saloon; John Unseld, Saloon, in this area in 1890's.
37. Prange Building at east corner of Lovell. (Remodelled in 1911.)
38. Chebra Benai Israel Synagogue on south side of South Street, across from Farmers Avenue. (After 1873.)
39. Kalamazoo Brewery at corner of Portage and Lake Streets. (Since 1878; today Kalamazoo Creamery.)

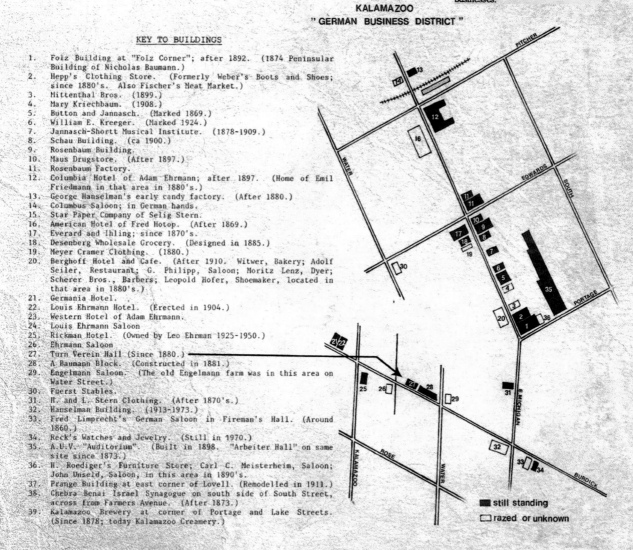

■ still standing
☐ razed or unknown

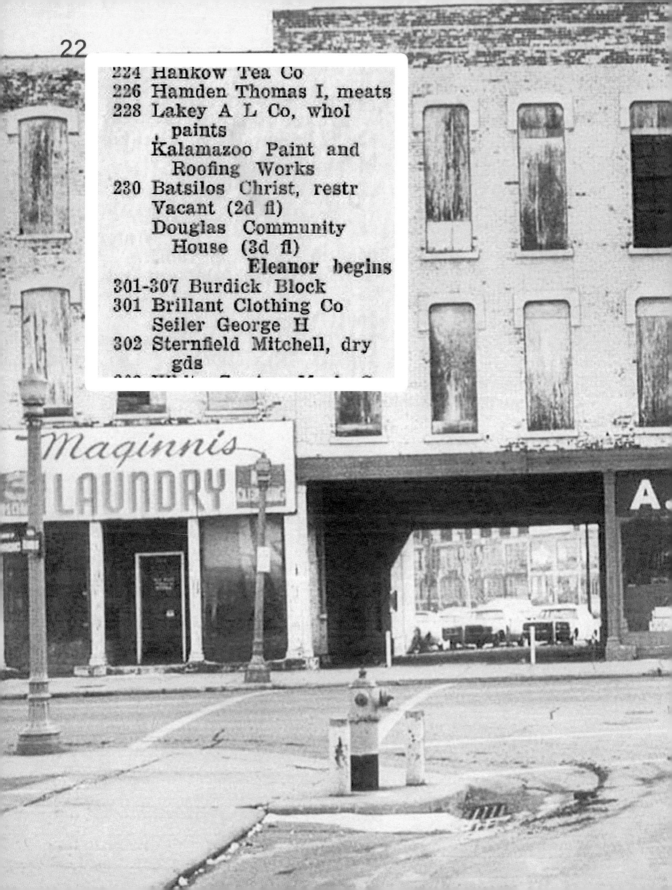

224 Hankow Tea Co
226 Hamden Thomas I, meats
228 Lakey A L Co, whol
    paints
    Kalamazoo Paint and
    Roofing Works
230 Batsilos Christ, restr
    Vacant (2d fl)
    Douglas Community
    House (3d fl)
            Eleanor begins
301-307 Burdick Block
301 Brillant Clothing Co
    Seiler George H
302 Sternfield Mitchell, dry
    gds

The original Turn Verein Hall became the home of A.L. Lakey's Paint Store and the Douglass Community Center (third floor). Preceding page: Map of German Business District circa 1900s.(Kalamazoo Public Library)

New Home for Soldiers

Simultaneously, as soldiers in Fort Custer came to train for war, Kalamazoo served as a safe haven for troops both Colored and White. White soldiers had their own place for respite at 121 West Main Street (now Michigan Avenue). Forrest Hill and his friends worked with prominent men to secure what would become the Frederick Douglass Community Center as a similar venue for Colored soldiers. The now-vacant five rooms on the third floor of Turn Verein Hall was the perfect place for the Colored soldiers. The main level of the building contained Lakey's Paint Store, and a laundry also was connected to the building.

Men enjoy a game of pool at the Douglass Community Center circa 1920s.
(Douglass Community Center Archives.)

Thanks to Forrest Hill, his friends, and members of the community, Colored soldiers had a place of recreation and community. The War Camp Community Services Board provided funds for furniture and other items needed to serve the soldiers. Behind the scenes, Colored and White residents worked together to make the Center a success, although with a unique leadership model. The organization was designed with a two-board model: a board of directors that was predominantly White and a predominantly Colored advisory board.

Just as the Douglass Center was becoming a reality, World War I ended on November 11, 1918. Soldiers began to be mustered out of Camp Custer. Those who remained as they awaited their next chapter in life continued to come to Kalamazoo; the need for a place of their own was still vital for the Colored soldiers. While the funds from the War Camp were no longer available, Forrest Hill and his friends kept the dream alive.

According to Kalamazoo Public Library's local history online article, "Douglass Community Association: The Northside Neighborhood Center," while the need to serve soldiers was the inspiration for the Center, the idea of a community center to serve all ages of the Colored population was born.

By 1919 the Turn Verein Hall's third floor space served well for the Frederick Douglass Community Center. The facility had plenty of room for dances, performances, and an audience capacity of more than four hundred. More importantly, many of the young men from small towns in Georgia, Kentucky, and Mississippi were away from home for the first time in their lives. They also had to adjust to the culture of the North. The women who volunteered to organize meals, snacks, card games, and dances for the men were invaluable.

First Director Creates Foundation

One of the first tasks of the newly created board was the search for the Center's first director. Pearl "Lottie" Mitchell came highly recommended. She was born in Wilberforce, Ohio, where her mother was a teacher and her father, Dr. Samuel Mitchell, was the second African American president of Wilberforce University. The university, created entirely for Colored students, was founded in 1856 and named for British abolitionist William Wilberforce.

Not only had Mitchell come from an educated family, they also were politically active. Dr. Samuel rescued the college from financial ruin when he partnered with the state of Ohio to secure public funds to support the university. His daughter joined the efforts of World War I and worked as a records clerk for Reserve Officer's Training Corps (ROTC) and then the War Camp Community Service at Hampton Institute in Virginia. Her training from Mary Church Terrell led to an assignment as the Girls' Worker for the Camp Community Service in Des Moines, Iowa. While in that role, she may have connected with Ernest T. Attwell, who served as Field Director for the Department of Colored Work, Playground and Recreation Association of America. Attwell would play a vital role in the formation of the Center's progress for years to come.

Mitchell, now 40 years old, was a perfect fit for the new Douglass Community Center. During her service as director, she created what would be the foundation of the organization—a soldier's club that included a place for all ages of the Colored community. In addition to her role as director, she was an active member of her sorority, Alpha Kappa Alpha Sorority, Inc. The sorority was founded in 1908 on the campus of Howard University in Washington, D.C., as the first Greek-letter organization founded by African American women. As a sorority member, Mitchell established the Mid-Western Region of the sorority and served as regional director before rising to national secretary.

In 1923 Mitchell left Kalamazoo for Ohio where she worked as a probation officer and investigator for Cuyahoga County Juvenile Court. In 1924 she was named the sorority's third international president and received recognition as membership director of the N.A.A.C.P.

Left: Pearl Mitchell in a portrait image. (akapioneers.aka1908.com)

Right: Mitchell accepts the Life Membership medal for the sorority from Dr. Wm. Lloyd Imes during the 1939 NAACP national convention in Richmond, Va. (*Crisis* Magazine)

Infant Welfare Station No. 1 was
located on Kalamazoo's Northside.
(Kalamazoo Public Library)

"It was in the war, and the young women often went there for dances, or to help the soldiers write letters home," said Dolly Brown Davis in an October 22, 1987, interview with the *Kalamazoo Gazette*. In the article, "They Helped Fight Loneliness," Davis, then 88, said how that first Community Center was a private organization that contributed to pride and belonging for not only the soldiers but the residents.

While the soldiers were still served, other groups in the community began to see the Hall as a meeting and social opportunity.

"I was in the study club," Davis continued, "which was a book study club. There were twenty-five women and a long waiting list. It was real restrictive. You have to be living in Kalamazoo three years before you could apply."

The community at large began to see the Center as a place that benefited Kalamazoo in more ways than one. In 1920, the organization separated from the War Camp Community Service leadership when the agency withdrew financial support. The Center formed its own independent organization and was incorporated. The following year they purchased the furniture and other equipment from the War Camp Community Service that had previously been purchased specifically for a club for soldiers.

The Community's Center

The organization was now standing solid on its own. People in the community began to take notice and credit it for a decrease in crime. One social work executive from the city, E.R. Hames, noted that the Center's presence "shows that comparatively, the Negroes of this city contribute a small number of cases to our courts and social agencies, a great deal of this credit should go to the Douglass Community

Center" (*Kalamazoo Gazette, 1930*). More importantly, the Community Fund of Kalamazoo (later the Community Chest and now United Way) felt the organization was worthy of grant funding. The Douglass Center now was in the league of nearly two dozen organizations such as the American Legion, Child Welfare League, Girl Scouts, Red Cross, Veterans of Foreign Wars, the Y.W.C.A, and the Y.M.C.A. who received annual funding to support their missions.

Above: A Men's quartet performs at Douglass Community Center, around 1920s. (Douglass Community Center Archives) Right: A brochure from Community Chest, 1928. (Kalamazoo Public Library)

Please

The description of the Douglass Community Center in the 1928 Community Chest annual giving report states:

Without this agency or one functioning in a similar way, the social and recreational status of the particular class it serves would not be the high standard maintained by our city. With it, the whole community is helped because of the help given a part of its population.

The organization's leaders played a vital role in the foundation of the Douglass Center.
- Earl Mitchell was the first president and board chairman. He served the organization for twenty-five years.

- Pearl Mitchell (no relation to the former Mitchell) was recruited from Cleveland to take the helm as the first executive director (1918-1924).

- A Mr. Miller served as executive director from 1924-26.

- Reverend Emory Barnes served as executive director 1926-1934. During this time Mr. Ernest T. Attwell from Philadelphia served as a consultant for organizations focused on the well-being of Colored people in the North and South. The Field Director for the Department of Colored Work, Playground and Recreation Association of America realized how vitally important recreation centers and playgrounds were to the mental and physical health of all people, particularly people of color.

Reverend Barnes' position in the community as pastor was vital, as ministers had influence and respect. In addition, the presence of Professor Ernest T. Attwell as a national leader in recreation for Colored people solidified the urgency to provide such opportunities in Kalamazoo. In a 1926 edition of *The American City* magazine, Attwell's article entitled "Recreation for Colored America" highlighted how dozens of communities in places such as Chicago, Saginaw, and Greenville, South Carolina, were examples of what happens when local philanthropists invest in their Colored citizens.

In the article, Attwell writes that the Bureau of Colored Work was created to "stimulate among Colored people an increase of opportunities for participation in local playground and recreation programs."

In keeping with this trend, Kalamazoo was also taking advantage of this opportunity to have organized places (indoors and outdoors) for recreation. Around this same time, local grocer Edward Desenberg (one of the consultants for the Douglass) was also an advocate of the fresh air models of recreation. In 1916, he founded Pretty Lake Camp on five acres in Mattawan. By the 1930s, that camp had grown to more than one hundred acres.

The mission of the Douglass Center was becoming broader than its founders had imagined. Plans were made to start summer camps for children while adding organized athletic competitions, music lessons and recitals, dances, games, arts and crafts and more. The community flocked to the Center, which soon resulted in overcrowding and overbooked programming. Turn Verein Hall's one-story accommodations were able to hold audiences up to four hundred; now that was no longer sufficient. In addition, the lack of elevators made accessibility a challenge for older residents, and heating was an issue in the winter as coal had to be carried up three flights to feed the coal stoves.

It was time for the organization to consider a larger facility, one they could build. In 1928, they found the perfect location on the corner of Ransom and Pitcher streets at a value of $11,000. This location was closer to the Northside where a majority of Colored residents were permitted to rent and own homes.

In 1929, the leadership solicited ideas for unique ways to raise the projected $40,000 needed to build their dream facility drawn up by local architect Ernest Batterson. One idea was to work with the city and apply for a grant. Another proposal was to raise funds through programs and bake sales. However, it was a recommendation by the Rev. Barnes that secured total support from the community and beyond.

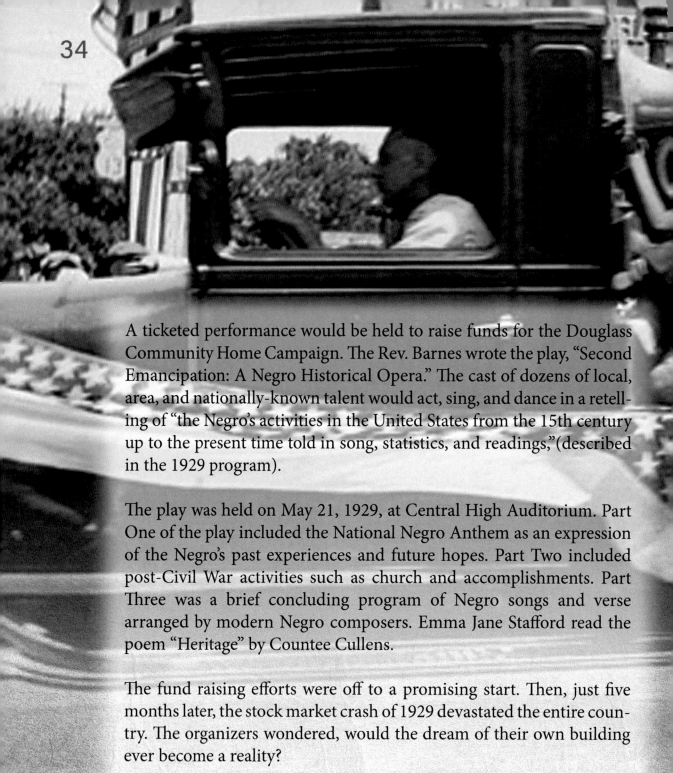

A ticketed performance would be held to raise funds for the Douglass Community Home Campaign. The Rev. Barnes wrote the play, "Second Emancipation: A Negro Historical Opera." The cast of dozens of local, area, and nationally-known talent would act, sing, and dance in a retelling of "the Negro's activities in the United States from the 15th century up to the present time told in song, statistics, and readings,"(described in the 1929 program).

The play was held on May 21, 1929, at Central High Auditorium. Part One of the play included the National Negro Anthem as an expression of the Negro's past experiences and future hopes. Part Two included post-Civil War activities such as church and accomplishments. Part Three was a brief concluding program of Negro songs and verse arranged by modern Negro composers. Emma Jane Stafford read the poem "Heritage" by Countee Cullens.

The fund raising efforts were off to a promising start. Then, just five months later, the stock market crash of 1929 devastated the entire country. The organizers wondered, would the dream of their own building ever become a reality?

The Douglass Community Center's Boys
Band took part in the Centennial Parade on
June 21, 1929. They are seen here passing
the Hathaway Tire Company at the corner
of West Main (now Michigan Avenue) and
Westnedge Avenue.
(Kalamazoo Public Library)

"I remember old Douglass and the time we spent camping at Eagle Lake. I recall the basketball team coached by Chester Taylor and the gals that played on it, Deany Duncan, Bernadine Earl, Della Gordon, Marybelle Jackson, Hennie Russell, and Vivian Dungy. I have fond memories of a club called the Les Chic Cheres. The refreshments we served after basketball games and the rented jukeboxes and the jam sessions. Those were the good old days." Vivian King

"Those were the good old days."

Making Memories

1930

DOUGLAS COMMUNITY ASSN CAMP

The Douglass Community Center was a place for African American men to participate in reading clubs and to discuss current events. (Douglass Community Association Archives)

When I went to work for the Douglass Community Association back in the '30s it was located on North Burdick and Eleanor Street in an old building up on the third floor. The third floor consisted of an office and lounge, a pool hall, a large room which was used as our auditorium and gym, a social-meeting room, and a kitchen of sorts.

There were pot-bellied stoves to keep warm in the winter. One of the more popular activities was on Friday or Saturday nights, especially when the Battle Creek teams were the opponents. I remember in particular the womanless wedding in which most of the men of the community took part. It was a gala affair. My father was a participant.

After many more memorable fundraising projects, we were able to finally build the structure on Ransom Street, of which we were all so very proud. It was dedicated in February 1941.

Marie Robinson
(Whaling Hawkins)

(Excerpts from the Frederick Douglass Community Association Grand Opening event program, 1984)

By the 1930s the Center was renamed the Douglass Community Association. Its mission had grown and its relevance in the community was vital to the prosperity of the nearly 970 Colored people in the city (an estimated 1,500 in the county). The Community Chest social fund organization provided much-needed dollars to the Douglass for its work in the community. Community Chest director George B. Rogers visited the North Burdick Street center and observed the need for more efficient accommodations in a more affordable rent district. He said, "(the Douglass is) heated by stoves and its plumbing and sanitary facilities are inadequate."

The Center continued to do the best with what it had, thriving as a model organization in the community. The Community Chest created a report, "What Welfare Federation Agencies Are Doing" in the *Kalamazoo Gazette* (October 31, 1930). Of the seventeen organizations the Chest provided funds to, the Douglass Center was noted as "the only organization in existence in Kalamazoo serving the educational and recreational needs of the poor colored person." The brief noted the Douglass on its services in areas of recreation, welfare services, and charitable services.

The Rev. Emory Barnes led as director of the organization from 1926 to 1934. His work expanded services and fund development needed to build a new center on the land purchased before the stock market crash of 1929. Barnes' battle with health issues led him to resign after eight of the most formative years.

Below:
A Womanless Wedding at the Douglass Community Center, 1936.

A nation-wide search began for a new director. E.T. Attwell, the field representative of the National Recreation Association in New York, facilitated the quest as he worked for a week in the community to assist with programming and the director search. The board and advisors agreed on Edward N. Powell of Syracuse, New York. Powell, with a background in social work, had served as director of the Dunbar Center. A community reception was held for him on August 1, 1934, at the Douglass Community Center.

He moved swiftly with creative programming and networked with community leaders. After just three years, his report to the Community Fund annual grant report boasted success. He shared how employment services now were added

Above: Ernest T. Attwell of the National Recreation Association stands in center of photo with Douglass board members circa 1930s. (Douglass Community Association Archives) *Note: Powell's correct initials are E.N.

to the social aspect of the organization that had come to serve all ages. The influence the Center had on the community was so strong that 1,265 people were on its mailing list, more than seventy-five percent of the Colored population of the county. Through their work, Powell reported an "attempt in no small way to improve the inter-racial attitude and conditions."

The Douglass Community Center was a home for the local Colored Boy Scout troop. (Douglass Community Association Archives)

According to his report in 1936, the Douglass provided 54 different activities for 744 individuals. The number of people and the activities they participated in included:

- Music classes, 75
- Drama, 46
- Handicraft, 57
- Children's hour, 89
- Boy Scout troop, 12
- Community night programs, 90
- Two-week camp through Y.M.C.A., 61 youth
- Swimming classes through City Recreation Department, 36 boys
- Dance classes, 47 youth

Powell reported of the more than 500 who attended the annual Christmas party and hundreds who attended everything from a Fall Bazaar to the Union Church Association's picnic at Milham Park.

Those outside the Colored community also took note of how the new Center was making a difference. Local social work executive E.R. Hames reported in a June 2, 1935, article that "a study made of juvenile delinquency in Kalamazoo shows that comparatively, the Negroes of this city contribute a small number of cases to our courts and social agencies. A great deal of credit for this record should go to the Douglass Community Center. It is our belief that the Douglass center gets as close to people who need its facilities as any social work set-up in the community."

The local Lucinda Hinsdale Stone chapter of the Daughters of the American Revolution (DAR) joined in to help raise the more than $40,000 for the newly proposed building on Ransom and Pitcher streets. In the article, "Douglass Center Benefit Garden Party Draws Crowd," the reporter shared how more than 500 came out to the event on a June evening (*Kalamazoo Gazette*, June 14, 1935). The benefit party was held in the adjoining yards of Mrs. Carl C. Blankenburg and Miss Irene Kleinstuck on Oakland Drive. The event committee included wives of prominent leaders such as Mrs. Lawrence H. Upjohn, women of the DAR, Kalamazoo Council of Federated Church Women, Kalamazoo Business and Professional Women's Club, and Kalamazoo Branch of American Association of University Women.

The fundraiser included a competition of goods baked by women from the Douglass. The official taste-testing judges included Mayor William Shakespeare, Jr., Stanley Morris, Jacob Kindleberger, E.W. Cade, Dunlap C. Clark, Ralph Hayward, and Carl C. Blankenburg. Their job was a challenge as they tasted a sunshine cake with orange icing by Mrs. Cora Ash, an angel food cake by Mrs. George Dungy, a lemon pie by Miss Virginia Walker, and a coconut cream pie by Mrs. Manuel. Candy, brownies, and rolls also featured on the judges' plates.

The winners received everything from $4 worth of groceries from Mrs. J. Stanley Gilmore to a knitting kit from Mrs. J.M. Alexander. The event went well into the evening, with music by the Upjohn orchestra and performances organized by participants of the Douglass. Douglass director Edward N. Powell concluded the event with thanks and appreciation to the DAR for their support.

It was clear the Douglass was a relevant part of the community. More than $22,000 had been raised locally, half of which was used to purchase the land on the corner of Ransom and Pitcher streets. To push along the dreams of a new location during the depression era, board members and advisors agreed to turn over the deed to the property and building to the City of Kalamazoo to apply for Public Works Administration (PWA) funds on behalf of the project. The National Industrial Recovery Act of 1933 was initiated during President Franklin Roosevelt's term. The first $3.3 billion in PWA funds would be used to build more than 30,000 highways, buildings, airports, military bases, bridges, dams, and other infrastructure in six years.

The leaders of the organization agreed to deed the site to the city, which would "turn over about $5,000 cash to form a contribution of approximately $16,000," according to the *Kalamazoo Gazette* article. With these funds, the City would apply for a grant of about $40,000 to build the structure. That plan would make the City the owner and would provide a long-term lease at a "nominal" rental to the Center.

State and local governments had the power to choose where they wanted to use the PWA funds and which contractors would be hired. The article "Douglass Center Turns Over Deed," reported $28,000 would be received from PWA funds to erect the new center (*Kalamazoo Gazette*, September 13, 1938).

THE DOUGLASS COMMUNITY CENTER
262 N. Burdick Street

1. Various organizations serve particular groups
of the city's population and among them is the
Douglass Community Center. Its primary effort is
to serve approximately 1800 colored citizens of
the City of Kalamazoo.

2. During the past year the Center made more direct
contacts with children and adults than at any other
time during its twenty years of serving the general
public from the standpoint of participation in
activities. 944 individuals took part in 42 listed
activities for a grand total attendance record of
32,000.

3. While the program is primarily character building
and recreational, the leadership is called upon to
perform many other duties and tasks in the general
field of social service.

4. During the year activities had to be carried
on outside of the Center. The program was curtailed
due to limitation of funds and inadequate facilities.

5. An Annual Bazaar attracted 18 clubs and organizations for a two day colorful festival. Many other
special events were sponsored during the year such
as; Annual Xmas Party, Open House program, basketball
games, Thanksgiving Union services and the annual
Union Picnic and Outing. The Center provided camping
opportunities for 23 girls, at Camp Norcum, Dexter,
Michigan, for two weeks and 52 boys at Camp Rota-
Ki-Wan, Bass Lake, for two weeks.

May 1939

Arrangements for the party were in charge of Mrs. Lawrence N. Upjohn, and she was assisted by a large committee of chapter members, and tickets were sold not only by the D. A. R., but also by the Kalamazoo Council of Federated Church Women, Kalamazoo Business and Professional Women's club, and the Kalamazoo branch, American Association of University Women.

6-14-35

Adequate Social Center For Negroes Looms Near

William Shakespeare, Jr., Vice Mayor, Leads Campaign to Raise Necessary Fund for Building.

1-12-36

The Douglass Community Center, an agency dedicated to the social, recreational and educational benefit of Kalamazoo's Negro population, will be housed in a fine new building if the plans and dreams of local citizens who have been interested in the organization can be worked out.

The Center, a Community Chest agency, was started as a meeting place for Negro soldiers stationed at Camp Custer in the immediate post war years, and was maintained later in five rooms on the third floor at 262 North Burdick street. The cramped quarters became increasingly inadequate with the years, and at present there is a pressing need for a new building.

William Shakespeare, Jr., vice mayor of Kalamazoo, has personally interested himself in the raising of funds required for the new structure, which will be erected at Ransom and Pitcher streets on a lot which the Center owns. The Negro organization has approximately $10,000 in cash. Shakespeare and others are attempting to raise an additional $12,000 by local subscription, which will make up the $23,000 local contribution of a proposed $40,000 WPA project to give the Center a new building.

TENTATIVE PLANS DRAWN

Tentative plans for the building have already been prepared by Ernest Batterson, local architect, and a clay model of the structure has been made.

Henry Powell, director of the Center, explains that a utilitarian building will be erected, designed to meet the needs of various groups, which include both boys and girls, young men and women and adults of all ages. The present quarters are altogether too small to meet the needs of such varied interests, Powell explains and he expresses the hope that provisions can be made for the new building as soon as possible.

The edifice will be somewhat modernistic in design, with large windows on all sides, providing plenty of interior natural light. A general purpose room, combining the features of auditorium and gymnasium, will be the largest in the building, measuring 51 by 72 feet. The stage will be 28 by 18 feet. Boys and girls locker rooms will be on opposite sides of the room. Other main floor side rooms will include a billiard room, a small kitchen, ladies rest room, and reading room. It is hoped that the excavation can be extensive enough to provide basement rooms for the boys activities.

THREE CLUB ROOMS

At the front of the building on the second floor will be three club rooms, each with a removable partition so that the three may be combined into one large room. This space is to be used for the various girls' activities. A second small kitchen will be adjacent to these rooms. Along the side of the building a lounge desk is contemplated, but it has not yet been definitely decided whether or not the lounge will be covered. It may take the form of an outdoor terrace. The general purpose room ceiling will extend to the roof.

Powell believes that the proposed building, with some changes may later become a reality. The Center is at present making a survey of the Negro population of the city, and Powell believes it to exceed 900 persons, the approximate 1930 census figure. Seven hundred different persons used the services of the Center last year, he reported.

The Center serves the Negro population in much the same fashion as the YMCA, the YWCA, and the Boy and Girl Scouts. Its activities among boys and girls are credited with limiting the juvenile delinquency rate in the Negro district of the city to a minimum, according to a Community Chest report issued last year.

ASSOCIATION PLANS EMPLOYMENT SERVICE

negro Kalc[?]

Formal opening of the Interstate Utility Service Association, organized here by E. M. Barnes to provide employment for Kalamazoo colored people, will be held next Saturday at headquarters of the group, 238 Bates court. This court connects Portage and Edwards street, running from Portage at the rear of the Leath Furniture store.

Some of the services rendered by the association will be shown at the opening. The place has been redecorated and included in the exhibits will be furniture repairing, painting and paperhanging, an auto wash rack and other services.

It is Barnes' plan to provide reliable service in many fields for Kalamazoo residents. Everything done is on the basis of satisfaction or no pay and only reliable workmen are employed.

Once under way here, Barnes expects to extend the plan to other cities.

9-23-37

PROMINENT GROUP ASSISTS

The activities of the Center are governed by a board of directors, comprised of Negro citizens, and an advisory board which includes seven white persons and six Negroes.

Shakespeare, now conducting the campaign for a $12,000 fund to make the new building possible, is a member of the advisory board, of which Dr. John Everett, Western State Teachers College, is chairman. John De Vries is vice chairman, Stanley Morris, treasurer, and Miss Irene Kleinstuck, secretary. Others include, Mrs. Dorothy U. Delano, Mrs. L. N. Upjohn, Mrs. [...]

Because the city had not secured the grant, all of the funds raised and the deed to the Center were returned to the organization. They would have to work without the city as their fiduciary agent and find other financial means to obtain the necessary funds to complete the project. Attwell attempted to motivate the board and advisors as reported in a May 12, 1939, article in the *Kalamazoo Gazette*, "Douglass Center Renews Drive."

"What the Douglass Community Association needs is such a small amount—less than $5,000 to complete its plan for a $60,000 project— it will be next to calamity to pass this opportunity over now," Attwell said.

Georgia Dungey was one of the most active members of the organization and took part in programs several days a week. Her oral history interviews throughout the years made no mention of the near dissolution of the plans for the new Center. She may have been too young to know the political aspects of the day, as her 1984 Douglass Souvenir booklet remarks recount only happy times.

Old Douglass meant reaching out to the community to help all ages. Story hour for the small children on Saturday, Forum on Sunday afternoon by college students, Girl's Unit on Wednesday, card party to help strangers become acquainted, Fall bazaar with clubs competing for the best-decorated booth, Friday night basketball games with boys and girls competing, and most of all the happy faces at the annual Christmas party. Each child received an article of clothing, a toy, a bag of candy, nuts and an orange.

Scrapbook of Douglass Community Association articles.
(Kalamazoo Public Library Local History Room)
Douglass sponsored Boy Scout Troop.
(Douglass Community Association Archives)

DOUGLASS COMMUNITY ASSOCIATION

262 N. Burdick St., Phone 4646

Mr. E. N. Powell, Ex. Secy.

39 or 40

It builds a better citizenship among the negro population through constructive employment of leisure hours. It provides a place for reading, discussion, forums, music, dramatics, athletic and social activities under trained supervision. Its program is confined primarily to recreational activities, both outdoor and indoor sports, but it also devotes much time in cooperating with other phases of social work, such as adjustment cases, calls for employment, job placements and contact with churches, fraternal and service organizations. It sponsors a boy scout troop which compares favorably with other scout troops in the city. Its rooms are used not only by organized but also unorganized groups. It seeks to give its boys and girls the benefit of summer camp life in so far as possible. It attempts in no small way to improve the inter-racial attitude and conditions.

It could easily carry on a much more comprehensive program with no increased expense or additional personnel if its rooms and facilities were more accessible and more nearly adequate.

Officers for the current year: Williams, H. A., Chairman; Earl, Frank, Vice Chairman; Hawkins, Mrs. Alice M., Secretary.

Services rendered during 1936: Provided 54 different activities for 744 individuals. Music classes, 75; dramatic, 46; handicraft classes, 57; children's hour program, 89; Boy Scout troop, 12; Community night programs, 90; a two-week camping period was provided for 61 boys and girls; through cooperation with Y.M.C.A. swimming classes were provided 36 boys; with the City Recreation department, dancing classes, 47 children.

Seven affiliated and outside clubs participated in a two-day Fall Bazaar, with an attendance of 356. A union Picnic, including church organizations and the association was held at Milham Park, attendance 375. Christmas party attendance 525. A banquet, honoring boy and girl athletes, Eddie Tolan, guest speaker, attendance 140.

The association rendered 12 outside programs, gratis; the Director was engaged for 24 speaking dates.

The association maintains a mailing list representing 1265 persons, better than three-quarters of the colored population, which is used extensively by individuals and outside organizations.

7

Proposed New Building for Douglass Community Center

If the PWA acts favorably upon applications of the City of Kalamazoo for a grant of approximately $25,000, Douglass Community's new home, shown in the architect's drawing above, will be a certainty. The city commission Monday night authorized City Manager Edward C. Kutz to make application for the grant, with the City of Kalamazoo acting as agent for Douglass Community. Sufficient funds have been subscribed locally to provide the building site in East Ransom street, and the balance of subscriptions are invested in bonds.

COMMISSION ACTS TO GIVE DOUGLASS CENTER NEW HOME

City Manager Authorized to Apply to PWA for Federal Grant.

Douglass Community Center, Kalamazoo's only organization devoted to the promotion of social, intellectual and recreational interest for the colored people of the community, Monday night reached a definite step nearer to a new home...

COST TO BE $48,000

Several years ago efforts were started to raise a fund of approximately $22,000 for Douglass Community Center, looking forward to a time when a modern home would be made available. Out of funds raised, approximately $12,000 was used for the purchase of the site in East Ransom street, the balance of the fund was invested in bonds.

The building site and the bonds have been made available to the City of Kalamazoo, and the site already has been transferred. The City of Kalamazoo will act as agent for Douglass Community Center in the project, which will involve a total expenditure of approximately $48,000, composed entirely of subscriptions and PWA grant.

Recent subscriptions to the Douglass Community Center building fund, raised primarily through efforts of Vice Mayor William Shakespeare, Jr., and other public spirited citizens, total to date about $32,000. This subscription fund will have to be increased approximately $3,700, to provide the necessary amount of local money necessary to carry through the project.

OUTGROWN ITS QUARTERS

He entertained no question but that the remaining quota of about $6,000 would be subscribed.

Douglass Community Center, formerly known as Douglass Community club, has long operated in Kalamazoo as a social and educational center for the colored population. It has occupied quarters upstairs at 262 North Burdick street.

Center activities have grown to such an extent that the present quarters are inadequate in size and facilities. Interests of the Center have been shouldered and promoted by many leading white citizens of Kalamazoo.

PWA Considers Application for Douglass Center

Water Softening Plant Aid Will Not Be Granted.

Reinstatement of the application to PWA for a grant with which to erect a new Douglass Community Center in Kalamazoo, at a cost of approximately $48,000, was assured the city commission Tuesday night in a telegram received from the regional director in Chicago.

Simultaneous with this assurance of consideration of the Douglass Community Center project, came an official notice from PWA that it will not consider applications for projects such as the proposed...

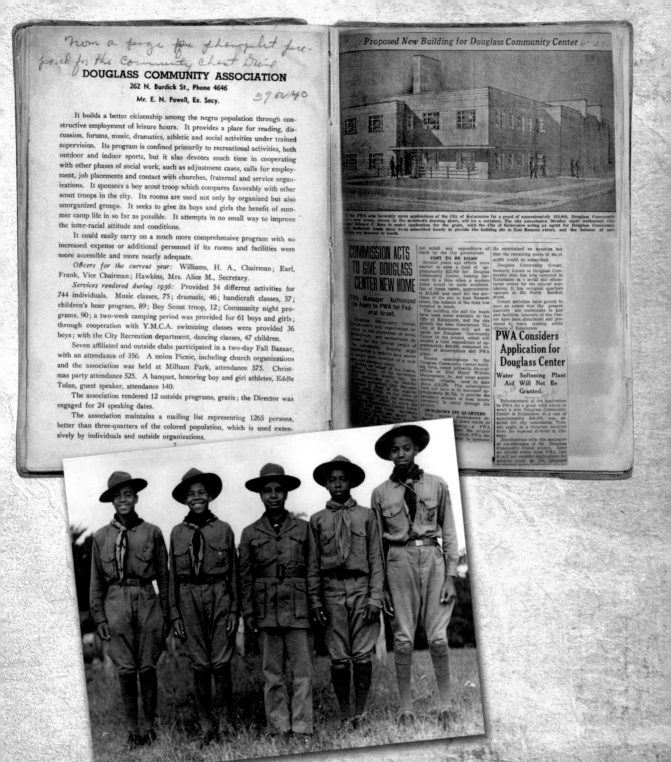

Efforts Continue Despite Depression

It was the unity that the Douglass brought to the Colored community that Alma Powell admired. She was born in Benton Harbor and lived on the East Side of Kalamazoo. In 1946 Powell would be known for her storytelling talents as the first African American library assistant in Kalamazoo. In 1938 she expressed the role the Douglass played in the community.

There are older organizations in the Negro community but after the churches, no other has rendered the widespread service as the Center, despite the harsh criticism and lack of cooperation it has labored under.

It served no particular clique or favors no particular church, it tried to seek out all people, particularly youth of color, and cater to them as far as their program will allow. It is trying, although it is a very hard job, to bring the Negro together as one large, cognizant, functioning group. The more churches there are, the more clubs, the more the group is split and scattered. But, the Center would like to bring all of the different units together. If they could accomplish this one aim, it would be a great service and a great feat.

Although the Great Depression plagued the country, the services and recreation provided by the Douglass offered a respite from the despair of soup lines and unemployment. Even in its cramped quarters on the third floor of the Turn Verein, Edward N. Powell continued to direct the Center's nearly fifty programs for close to 1,000 youth and adults.

The constant traffic of the Douglass Community Association and the A.L. Lakey Paint Store on the street level of the building made a perfect location for Charles Pratt, a young attorney, to open his law practice. Charles, one of eight children of Otis Pratt, graduated from Kalamazoo Central High School in 1928. He left Michigan and headed to Howard University in Washington, D.C., where he earned

a degree in law. Upon gradu-ation in 1935, he returned to his hometown to practice and serve as a board member of the Douglass, an organiza-tion his father helped envi-sion with friend Forrest Hill. Charles' practice thrived and he married Thelma (Lenox). However, in 1939, before he could begin to enjoy life as a newlywed, he was called to serve as an infantry officer in World War II.

Those of all ages enjoyed the warmth of the coal-burning furnace of the original Douglass Community Center, around 1930s.(Douglass Community Association Archives)

In the meantime, Powell did his best to lead the organiza-tion. But with the war in effect and Pratt not around to help with legal matters, the Douglass was evicted from their home after nearly 20 years as occupants. Powell worked with other agencies such as the Child Welfare League to ensure youth programming continued in areas throughout the city. Camping opportunities dwindled due to lack of funds, support for the annual bazaar, sports activities, and dances lacked participation due to inadequate space in the community to house them. A temporary office at 139 E. Michigan Avenue would have to suffice as they attempt-ed to keep things as close to normal as possible. But the future of the Douglass and all Powell had built was in limbo.

Opportunities to participate in team sports and musical ensembles were a draw to the Douglass Community Center for African Americans who were often barred from playing in other organizations due to segregation.(Douglass Community Association Archives)

54

"I was fortunate in having been given the opportunity to organize the Douglass Nursery school in 1941 and to serve as headteacher. Some of the happiest days of my life happened there. Occasionally I met some of the former students and it gives me a feeling of pride and fulfillment."

Myrtle Rouse

"*It will always be special.*"

Starting Anew

1940

I cannot remember a time when I did not go to "The Center." My mother took me there on Thursday afternoons when she went to meet with her clubs and friends. As I grew, the Center became my place, too. Parties...summer camp...dance class...music, plays, programs, clubs, afternoon teas...

The Douglass not only provided my recreation, it provided me with my first job experience (as an) after school counselor and activity director/summer camp leader, and also let me meet the man of my life there. The Douglass means much to me and there is a bond to all the people of Kalamazoo that is unique and unseverable. It was special, IT IS SPECIAL, and it will always be special.

Betty Maxwell Williams
(Remembrances from the 1984 Douglass Community Association Souvenir Booklet)

A teen queen is celebrated for selling the most tickets to a dance. (Douglass Community Association Archives)

Director Edward N. Powell was challenged to maintain camaraderie in the community while operating in a temporary facility. The eviction from their North Burdick location after more than twenty years meant a focus toward a permanent site. At the same time, he had to maintain optimism about the building of a new center while securing funds to build. His desire for a permanent center was expressed in the article "Douglass Center Activities Have Difficult Year."

"Much effort to find temporary quarters for an effective program has been spent, but to no avail" (*Kalamazoo Gazette*, January 4, 1940).

It was evident that two separate advisory boards helped create the Douglass, one White and one Colored. They shared a goal to create a beautiful facility of recreation, educational, and employment advancement. One of the champions of that effort was Edward Desenberg. He had been one of the community leaders approached by Forrest Hill and his friends to help find a solution to the lack of social opportunities in Kalamazoo for the Colored soldiers. As plans were made to break ground on the new center site, the community was struck with sad news. Desenberg had died on January 20th at a Chicago hospital. He was 72. Not only would those of the Douglass mourn his death, but also those who knew him as the founder of Pretty Lake Vacation Camp for underprivileged children in Kalamazoo.

How Douglass Community Center Building Will Look When Completed

How the new Douglass Community Center building is expected to look when it is completed about the middle of June. It will be located on the northwest corner of East Ransom and North Pitcher streets. Work will be formally started at 11 Saturday morning when former Mayor William Shakespeare, Jr., turns over the first spade full of dirt, in the presence of city officials and state representatives of the WPA, co-sponsor of the project. The $54,000 building is to be used by the city's colored population.

Breaking Ground

Former Kalamazoo Mayor William Shakespeare, Jr., was at the historic ground-breaking ceremony on February 17, 1940. As one of the men on the front line of the building effort, he sacrificed a few days of his winter retreat in Florida to take part in an event that had been developing for a decade. Finally, the community could celebrate the groundbreaking of a new Center. The winter-hardened soil did not prevent Shakespeare and nearly one hundred other community members and leaders from bundling up to take part in the ceremony.

The ceremony included testimonies from Earl Mitchell, president of the "Negro" board. Mitchell called the project a true community enterprise "because contributions came from people in every walk of life and ranged from 20 cents to $2,000" (*Kalamazoo Gazette*, February 18, 1940).

A 1941 article in the Kalamazoo Gazette highlights the building plans for the new Douglass Center on Ransom Street. (Kalamazoo Public Library Local History Archives)

The first turn of the soil was by Advisory Board Chairman Shakespeare, followed by Mayor Frank E. McAllister, City Manager Edward S. Clark, Public School Superintendent of Building and Chief Engineer John DeVries, Mrs. Irene Kleinstuck, Mrs. L.N. Upjohn, and Stanley Morris, who served as master of ceremonies. Board of directors member Henry A. Williams also was in attendance at the ground breaking of the estimated $70,000 project.

In the meantime, programs for youth and adults continued to thrive. Director Powell had kept the organization running as smoothly as possible in his nearly seven years at the helm. Construction had begun on their new location in March of 1940, and while they watched the progress, students and adults still needed a place of recreation and employment resources. The temporary facility at 139 East Michigan Avenue had to suffice. It was there that parents came to sign up girls and boys for summer camps at Rota-Kiwan on Bass Lake or Camp Norcum in Dexter, Michigan. A boys' band was

After years of challenges to raise funds, members of the integrated Douglass Community Association board break ground on the new building site. (Douglass Community Association Archives)

founded and donated instruments contributed to the cause.

The impact the Douglass had on lowering crime in the city had been commended by Welfare authorities. The Douglass and the Third Street Community Center served minority groups in the city. Third Street worked with Hungarians and Polish residents as well as those who sought to complete their education. Because both organizations were in dire straits for funding to continue their work, a football game between the Chicago Bears and St. Louis Gunners was arranged as a fundraiser. The two community organizations would split the funds from the game to be held in September of 1940 at Waldo Stadium.

Keys to the Douglass

The funds from donors and fundraisers were essential to the completion of the building. Those who had resources or connections used them to help the Center. Congressman Paul W. Shafter of Battle Creek used his political clout to secure $2,046 in supplemental funds from the Work Progress Administration (WPA) for flooring, heating, electrical, plumbing, and plastering walls (*Kalamazoo Gazette*, November 22, 1940).

Edward N. Powell, the organization's fourth executive director, solicits funds for the new building in this historic document that pictures images of the newly-built Center. (Kalamazoo Public Library)

Professional Football Game to Benefit Two Settlement Projects

Douglass and Third Street Community Centers Will Share in Proceeds.

9-12-40

Kalamazoo's two most active settlement projects will benefit from the first professional football game in this city, to be played Saturday afternoon at Waldo Stadium between the Chicago Bears and the St. Louis Gunners.

Both the Douglass Community Center and the Third Street Community Center are badly in need of building funds. In fact, the decision of the sponsoring Junior of Commerce to divide the net proceeds of the game between the two settlements is a "God-send," settlement workers said.

Each of the welfare projects has been long established in Kalamazoo. The Douglass Community Association is out of money in the midst of a fine program. A fine, n_____ _____derway a___ the r_____ _____ast Ra____ som_____ _____reets ___ a fe_____ _____ort _____

completion, and the building fund has been exhausted.

Faced with Discontinuance

On the other hand, the Third Street center, conducted for about 20 years at 1206 Third street by various Kalamazoo churches faced the prospect of being discontinued about the first of this year when the churches felt they could no longer support it.

The Council of Social Agencies and some of its affiliated welfare groups came to the Third Street center's rescue. They re-organized it and set it up on a temporary basis, hoping that after a year of operation it will be given assistance by the Community Chest, ___ _____ ____ settlements ren_____ ____undreds of Kala___ ____ their respective _____nter, founded

about the time of the United States entry into the World war, has been the one outstanding project for aid to the city's Negro people. By the hundreds they have come to the center year after year, in first one old building and then another, for recreational activities, for education, for care of babies and small children, and for religious leadership.

The Third Street center has provided a similar program for the many alien people in its neighborhood. Many of them are Hungarians, others are Polish. Many are American-born people who never had a chance to complete their education or participate in school and church social life.

Seen Crime Deterrent

Welfare authorities throughout the district are unanimous in their approval of both of these projects. In the Douglass center work, Kalamazoo has been held up as an example for the nation to follow. The police authorities indorse these projects as the best kind to lower crime standards and promote better understanding.

The people who attend these centers are doing as much as they can to promote the football game, which they realize may give them a new lease on life—or may even mean the difference between the continuance or closing of this work. From work-hardened adults to youngsters still in grammar school, they are out making posters advertising the game, placing them in store windows throughout the community, and selling tickets to the game.

Several of Kalamazoo's larger industrial firms have recognized the value of the settlements receiving a sizeable share of the proceeds and have bought blocks of tickets to the game. Some of these are being resold to employes and some are being given away.

The Kalamazoo Gazette featured this football event held to support the Douglass and other community youth-serving organizations. (Kalamazoo Public Library)

ALL PRO
CHICAGO BEARS
VS.
ST. LOUIS GUNNERS
Charity Football Game
WALDO STADIUM
KALAMAZOO, MICHIGAN
Sat. Sept. 14   2:30 P. M.
ALL SEATS RESERVED
$1.10 $2.20

Nearly one year after the groundbreaking ceremony, on Sunday, February 16, 1941, the community was invited to the Dedicatory Exercise of the Douglass Community Association at 231 East Ransom Street. According to the article, "New Douglass Center Opened at Ceremonies," nearly 700 people, White and Colored, took part in the three hours of speeches to celebrate the momentous occasion (*Kalamazoo Gazette*, February 17, 1941).

Grandpa Forrest Hill (Pauline Byrd Johnson's grandfather who proposed a much-needed place for Colored soldiers in 1919) suffered a heart attack in 1937 and died at age 85. There is no recorded mention of him at the ceremony where 75 Negro soldiers from Fort Custer joined those from throughout the Midwest to celebrate the collaborative efforts of a community. Hill would have been proud of what evolved from their kitchen table talk in 1919. He also would have been proud of the speech presented by E.T. Attwell, director of the Bureau of Colored Work for National Recreation Association. Attwell came from his New York office to be a part of what Hill's efforts had helped accomplish.

Pauline remembered her grandfather had insisted that not all Negroes had been slaves. Attwell's keynote address supported Forrest's declaration and lifted up the role of the Negro soldier in America. Attwell also gave credit to the role the race had played in other aspects of the country's progress from education to science. He also commended the organization's leaders on allowing the legacy of Frederick Douglass to be immortalized in the name, calling Douglass "one of the greatest single influence for good in the history of the American Negro."

The idea of a place for soldiers and community, coupled with the beautifully designed building, was an effort people across the country admired and attempted to emulate. After a denial of funds from the

Public Works Administration (PWA), a successful initiative was undertaken to secure construction and labor support through the Work Progress Administration (WPA). The WPA was created by President Franklin D. Roosevelt as part of his New Deal to get the people of America working again during the worst period of the Great Depression (www.history.com, "Works Progress Administration.")

The WPA workers' diligence led to the completion of the structure in less than a year from the groundbreaking ceremony. The vision the director and board had for the Douglass was one to behold. Its modern three-story brick complex would include a large gymnasium, library, social rooms, and snack bar.

The rollercoaster of financial woes, evictions, and challenges to continue business as usual in temporary quarters all seemed worthwhile as a litany of speakers, presentations, and performances honored the new building. Dr. C.A. Alexander, the city's first Negro doctor, was the emcee for the event. Mayor Frank Mcallister presented a greeting and City Manager Edward Clark presented the building keys to Douglass Board President Earl C. Mitchell.

Former Mayor William Shakespeare, Jr., had welcomed the chance to provide a place for Colored soldiers when approached by Hill and his friends in 1919. His efforts to garner support and raise funds had been a true labor of love that led to nearly $22,000 in cash being raised by the community. With the $30,000 in WPA labor funds added to the total, Shakespeare was overwhelmed that the nearly 20-year battle to secure the property and building had been won. He was so emotional during the event that when asked to speak, he could only say, "I'm too happy to talk," and took his seat.

An article in the Kalamazoo Gazette shows the new library in the Douglass Center. A dance for soldiers from Fort Custer are among the images in the Douglass Community Association archives.

The Douglass Community Center Association will formally accept its $70,000 new home at 231 East Ransom street today. Here are three interior views of the modern new building: Top Left—The information desk in the lobby. Top Right—The spacious East Clubroom. Below — The library, where Victor Tate, Ray Johnson, and Ed Walker are exploring.

E. N. Powell, left, director of the Douglass Center, and Earl Mitchell, veteran president of the association, will participate in today's program.

Social Time, War Time

The opening of the new Douglass could not have come at a better time for a new era of soldiers. The Selective Training and Service Act had been signed by President Franklin D. Roosevelt in 1940 and by January of 1941, nearly 11,000 Kalamazoo County men had enlisted in the draft. A recorded 54 of them were sent for training at Camp Custer. Women of the Douglass formed the War Wives' Club to provide everything from meals to letter-writing services to the families of soldiers, and to soldiers who had been deployed.

In addition to serving soldiers, the new building provided the space needed to provide quality services to those of the Colored community. Immediately, ideas for new youth programs were shared. Vivian King had participated in story time at the original Douglass above Lakey's Paint store on North Burdick Street. Now, as a teenager, she and her friends formed clubs such as the Girls Unit and Las Amigas.

African-American US Army Captain Camp Columbia, Brisbane, Australia, 29 Jun 1943. Photographer: Harold Hoffman Source: ww2dbaseUnited States Army Signal Corps

The social clubs provided the young women an opportunity to show their leadership skills and support to the organization. The Las Amigas raised $600 to purchase a mimeograph copy machine and furnished one of the upstairs rooms.

Seventeen Colored Children Enrol in Town Camp

KAL- G- 6-29-42

Seventeen colored children 6 to 13 years old, enrolled in Douglass Community Center's second annual "Town Camp," this morning. The camp, designed to provide recreational activities for colored children who otherwise would not enjoy these privileges, will continue for six weeks.

Shown above is the initial group that opened camp today, with the directors and supervisors in the rear row. They are, left to right, E. N. Powell, director of Douglass Community Center, Miss Delma Warfield, Miss Julia Powell, general supervisor, Miss Georgia Price, and Charles Thomas. Elwood Madison, another supervisor, was not present when the picture was taken.—Gazette Photo.

Below: The Douglass Community Association was housed in this Ransom Street building from 1941-1984. (Kalamazoo Public Library-Mamie Austin Collection)

They competed among themselves to see who could get the most dime votes. In addition, they crowned the winner of the challenge at a dance where participants paid a fifty cent entrance fee.

The Douglass Center became the place for community dances for all ages. Whether parents danced to the big band music of Tommy Dorsey and Duke Ellington or youth bounced to the jitterbug bouncing beats of Cab Calloway and Art Tatum, the gym was perfect. Women danced with soldiers dressed in their military uniforms and the best jitterbug dancers ruled the floor. The balcony that overlooked the gym was also the ideal place for a full view of the action.

Finally, since the closing of the original Douglass, there was room again for the highly-anticipated annual Christmas bazaars held on the first Friday and Saturday of December. Various organizations, churches, and individuals hosted tables to sell everything from desserts to homemade crafts.

Called to Duty

The soldiers from Fort Custer always volunteered to return on Sunday after the bazaar to help clean up and store tables and chairs. After the first bazaar in December of 1941, Vivian King remembered the soldiers from Fort Custer who came to help clean the gym. She also remembered how the director, Edward N. Powell, ran

Duke Ellington's hits such as "Satin Doll" and "Sophisticated Lady" were often played during early dances at the Douglass. (http://www.defenseimagery.mil)

from his home on Edwards Street (a block away). He was in a panic. He had received a call from the military base ordering the soldiers to return immediately. The men assured him they had permission to be there, but Powell had received a call from the base. It was Sunday, December 7, 1941, and the Japanese had just bombed the U.S. Naval Base in Pearl Harbor, Hawaii.

The entire country had been informed about the attack by radio. Residents of Kalamazoo heard the news on WKZO, the station created by John Fetzer just ten years earlier. The station was housed in the Burdick Hotel and was a source of entertainment and news for the community. It was during a Sunday afternoon broadcast of the Philharmonic Orchestra of New York that the announcement of the bombing shocked the nation.

Many of the soldiers, whose only sense of home was the Douglass, were deployed to fight the Japanese. The women had already said goodbye to other soldiers who were among the millions mobilized to fight in Europe and now in the Pacific. The War Wives committee would keep their promise to write and send care packages, just as they had for World War I soldiers of Camp Custer. While some soldiers married local women or kept in contact after the war, there were others the women never heard from again. After the war, it would be reported that sixty-one men from Kalamazoo County lost their lives in action.

The purpose for which the organization was founded, to serve Colored soldiers, changed after World War II. There were fewer soldiers trained at Camp Custer after the war, and the Colored community in Battle Creek formed its own version of the Douglass, the Hamblin Community Center. In addition, the interurban

Visitors Day for the 184th Field Artillery at Camp Custer, Michigan, brings thousands of Chicagoans to the Army post to inspect the equipment and meet their friends and relatives. Camp Fort Custer, Michigan, June 1941. (http://www.army.mil/cmh/topics/afam/earlyWW2.htm)

transportation system that had once brought thousands of soldiers into the community was defunct. The reason for the Douglass was beginning to shift.

A New Focus

In 1942, a Better Citizenship Council was incorporated to sponsor youth and citizen education at the Douglass after they learned of a kindergarten class held at the Center.

Director Edward N. Powell had organized efforts to send dozens of youth to camp each summer. Now, their new facility allowed for day camps, called Town Camp, right on the premises. Under the leadership of Julia Powell, youth ages 6 to 13 who were not able to participate in away-from-home camp experiences attended the six-week Town Camp. Each day they took part in a drama class, music lessons, and organized arts and crafts.

To expand their horizons youth also were taken on picnics, hikes, and tours to such places as Wolf Lake Hatchery, the Kellogg Bird Sanctuary, and Milham Park (*Kalamazoo Gazette*, June 29, 1942).

The success of the Douglass was evident under Powell's leadership. Those across the country took notice of what neighborhood support could do to benefit its Colored citizens. Others wanted that same success for their communities and Powell was highly sought after to do the job. In December of 1944, after eleven years of seeing the Douglass through trials and triumphs, he left the community for Stanford, Connecticut, to work for a similar community organization.

No time was wasted to find a replacement for Powell. The board appointed 41-year-old Edward Lewis as the new director in the spring of 1945. He and his family moved from Farrell, Pennsylvania, into the home that Powell had formerly occupied at 725 North Edwards Street. Lewis had served as director of a community center in Farrell and had a history working for boys' clubs in New York and Pittsburgh. The board was attracted to Lewis for his vision to provide premier summer activities for youth. However, Lewis' appointment was short-lived as he accepted a position with Superior Life Insurance Company in Detroit.

John Ridley of Ft. Wayne, Indiana, replaced Lewis in 1946 but would not remain more than a year before taking a job in Ithaca, New York. In the meantime, volunteers and dedicated community leaders helped keep the ship afloat. The vision to equip youth for the present and future was always at the forefront of staff and board. In 1946, Kathryn Wallace of Illinois was hired to serve as assistant director and director of the girls' activities. The following year Frederick Douglass Jefferson of Bramwell, West Virginia, was hired as the boys' director with plans to create camera and woodworking clubs and supervise athletic activities.

That same year a major step in race and community relations occurred at the Douglass. "Although many changes took place at Douglass during its first 20 years, none were greater than those which took place in 1946," said Pauline Johnson in her article, "The Beginning: Douglass Community Association Through the Eyes of Pauline Johnson." Her reflection in the 1984 Souvenir Program for the Frederick Douglass Community Association applauded the move in 1946 to change the Center bylaws to create one board, not two separate boards of White and Colored leaders. This shift allowed for a more unified vision of the Douglass and who would best fit as director.

Dances, concerts, and plays were held on the stage in the Center's gymnasium. Performers from across the country entertained the locals as did collaborative lecture series events that included nationally-known presenters and music from such churches as the Mt. Zion Baptist Church choir. A grand celebration to ring in 1947 with a New Year's Eve party was planned by members such as Alma Powell, Maxfield LeCompt, and Myrtle Rouse. Adults would revel at the Snowball Party from 10 p.m. to 2 a.m. By September of 1947, Kalamazoo native Lee Roy Pettiford was interviewed and named director of the Douglass. The board hoped Pettiford would bring stability to an organization in much need of a dedicated leader.

Pettiford's resilience, as much as his accomplishments as an adult, was impressive. Not only had Pettiford's mother died when he was seven, but his father Joe, a custodian at Kalamazoo City Hall, died when Pettiford was 13 years old. Joe, along with Forrest Hill, Otis Pratt, Taylor Burnett, and Joe Small, were the men who had desired a place for Colored soldiers in 1919. Pettiford's own father helped bring the idea of the Douglass Community Association to life.

Pettiford did not allow his beginnings as an orphan to define his future. He became an athletic stand-out at Kalamazoo Central High School and worked to save money. Upon graduation in 1934, he enrolled in Wilberforce University, where he earned a Bachelor of Science in Social Administration in 1940. He returned home to take graduate classes at Western Michigan College (now Western Michigan University) and went on to join the others drafted to serve in the military during World War II. After three years in the service, he returned home as a sergeant.

It was clear that a young man from Kalamazoo could best relate and have a commitment to those in his community, particularly youth. He knew the importance of mentorship and education. In a letter to the membership the board said about Pettiford:

"We feel that it is of decided inspiration to other young people to see one who has grown up here, attended Central High School, finished college, and then returned to this community in a dignified, responsible, respected position such as the direc-torship of Douglass Center represents."

The archives of the Douglass Community Association includes program booklets, photographs, and documents that highlight decades of events.

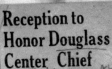

Miss Kathryn Wallace
—Gazette Photo

Reception to Honor Douglass Center Chief

Sunday Event for Edward Lewis, New Director.

A public reception honoring Edward R. Lewis, newly appointed director of Douglass Community Center, and his family, will be held from 4 to 7 Sunday afternoon at the center by the board of directors of Douglass Community Association, assisted by the auxiliary clubs.

Lewis succeeded Edward N. Powell who resigned last January to accept a position in New York state. He is married and has two sons, Edward, Jr., 12, and Ronald, 10. He is making his home at 725 North Edwards street, where the Powells formerly resided.

Native of Kentucky

Lewis is 41 years old and a native of LaGrange, Ky. He received his education in Pittsburgh and New York City, and specialized in sociology and boys' club work at the New York University. For nine years he was director of the Kay Boys' club at Pittsburgh, and for four and one-half years was director of the community center at Farrell, Pa., which position he resigned to accept the directorship of Douglass Center.

Pleased with Local Center

His appointment to the Kalamazoo position was announced by Earl C. Mitchell, president of Douglass Community Association, the Rev. Bernis E. Warfield, chairman of the board of directors, and William Shakespeare, Jr., chairman of the advisory board.

Among his first efforts Lewis now is planning the summer activities program for the center. He stated that Kalamazoo has one of the best, if not the best, colored community center in the United States.

Douglass Center Adds Director

Reception Sunday for 2 New Staff Members.

Appointment of Miss Kathryn Wallace, 713 North Edwards street, as assistant director of Douglass Community Center, and director of girls' activities, was announced today by the board of directors and by Earl C. Mitchell, president of the Douglass Community Association.

Miss Wallace became affiliated with Douglass Community Center last Dec. 1, coming here from Champaign, Ill., where she was director of a service center. She has had several years experience in community activities.

Edward E. Lewis, 41, was appointed director of Douglass Community Center March 18, coming here from Farrell, Pa., where he was director of a community center for four and a half years.

A public reception in honor of Director Lewis and Assistant Director Wallace will be sponsored by directors at Douglass Center from 4 to 7 next Sunday afternoon. A previous reception was postponed because of the death of President Roosevelt.

> "I remember working at the Douglass as an executive secretary under the directorship of Mr. Lee Roy Pettiford. I can yet visualize kids playing basketball in the gym, directed by Mr. John Caldwell, and girls participating in arts and crafts. The Douglass was fully utilized with a host of meetings, dances, parties, and other community functions. The atmosphere displayed there was friendly. I had the opportunity of meeting a lot of people. The experience was most rewarding."
>
> Patsy Jones

"*Meeting the needs of the individuals in the community.*"

A Home Away From Home

1950

The Douglass Community Association will always be a part of my life. My first professional job as girls' worker was at the Douglass. The challenge of the job enticed me to stay for six years. Kalamazooans are my friends and hold a special place in my heart. Most of all I met my husband Robert "Al" Goodwin at the Douglass.

Juanita (Overby) Goodwin was the first Black female principal for Kalamazoo Public Schools. Al Goodwin became the first Black police officer to retire from the Kalamazoo Police Department in 1976.

These young campers take a break from city life to enjoy nature during Douglass summer camp opportunities at area lakes and cabins. (Douglass Community Center Archives)

In 1950, the country was recovering from World War II. The efforts of the women of the War Wives' club slowed. They no longer needed to take the lead to ensure Colored soldiers from their community and Fort Custer had support or organize letter-writing sessions to soldiers. No longer was there a need to assemble care packages of treats, magazines, and notes of encouragement. Dances held to take their minds off deployments slowed, and some local women married soldiers who were among the many bachelors.

The Douglass Community Association maintained its dedication to soldiers through dances, access to resources, and letter-writing campaigns to G.I.s who served overseas. (Douglass Community Association Archives)
Soldiers read letters from home. (www.defense.gov)

Baby boomers were growing up in a world that was ready for peace and prosperity after decades of war and the Great Depression. In Kalamazoo, toddlers left their mothers' sides for a few hours of the day to take part in nursery school at the Douglass. Their little feet ran in a gym that for them may have seemed as big as a football field. Teens giggled as they skipped through the Douglass to take part in sewing classes or music lessons. In the evenings, girls' and boys' basketball teams competed against neighboring communities, and all hustled to the snack bar where sodas and snacks awaited.

Adult clubs such as the Masons, Elks, and the American Legion and its auxiliaries met for meetings and social events. As one of the most modern and centrally-located centers in the community, other organizations such as the Red Cross, Council of Churches, the Boy Scout Council, and other social agencies reserved the Douglass for training and events.

An annual membership drive led by Elizabeth Purchase secured five hundred members, a record for the organization. More than one hundred students registered for the summer day camp, and overnight camps at Lake Michigan were planned. Director Lee Roy Pettiford had led the organization in a direction so successful that visitors locally and nationally came to tour the facility.

In 1950, the integrated board worked together to provide the financial and organizational support needed for success.

In a September 9, 1951, *Kalamazoo Gazette* article, one local leader and businessman offered praises to the organization.

Star Paper Company manager Neil Schrier said, "I'd like to recommend a visit to the Center by anyone who has any question about its work or its accomplishments. My tour there was most educational."

Douglass to Open Camping Roles Monday

Maximum Enrolment to Be One Hundred.

Registration for Douglass Community Association's Day Camp will open tomorrow at Douglass Center and continue until June 24. The maximum enrolment will be the first 100 children registered by their parents. The camp will be open to children 7 to 14 years of age.

Douglass Community Association will sponsor a five-weeks Day Camp this year, opening June 26 and continuing until July 28, with weekly camp periods Monday through Friday from 9:30 a.m. to 4:30 p.m.

ADVISORY COMMITTEE

The camp advisory committee, composed of Mrs. Charles Pratt, chairman, the Rev. Bernis Warfield, Jr., Mrs. LaRue White, Mrs. Emerson Mitchell, Mrs. Bernice Cox and Mrs. James Baker, has made plans to assist the camp personnel in promoting, planning and providing specialized information on health examinations, transportation and over-night camping.

Cost per child for the five-weeks camp has been held to a minimum to make it possible for the largest number of children to receive camping experience.

PLAN OVERNIGHT CAMPS

Through co-operation of the American Red Cross and the city recreation department swimming will be made available two days a week. A visiting librarian from the Kalamazoo public library will conduct story-telling periods once each week. Two over-night camp programs have been scheduled, one for Van Buren State park on Lake Michigan, and the other at a local park.

The unique leadership model of an interracial board that worked together for the needs of Colored residents was one to be admired. The organization founded with the sole purpose of providing a social outlet for Colored soldiers had evolved into more than its founders could have imagined.

As wartime efforts subsided, the Douglass placed heavy focus on youth-centered activities. (Douglass Community Association Archives)

Douglass Drive Opens Wednesday

Community Association to Seek New Members.

The annual membership drive of the Douglass Community Association will open Wednesday, May 10, and continue until May 31.

Membership in the association is open to all who desire to support activities sponsored by the association, which include programs to meet the spiritual, welfare, and recreational needs of every person in the community without regard for race or creed.

Founded in 1919, Douglass Community Association is a member of the National Recreation Commission and is a Red Feather agency. It is governed by a biracial board of directors that meets monthly. Members of this board are Charles Williams, president; Mrs. Mary McKellar, vice president; Mrs. Norma Cash, secretary; Alden Byrd, treasurer; and Mrs. Sallie Graine, Miss Elizabeth Purchase, Mrs. Alma Powell, Mrs. Edith Williams, Dr. D. V. Estill, Robert Sutton, Jr., Walter Ware, A. B. Connable, Jr., Lawrence Mitchell, Mrs. Clio Van Valkenburg, and Charles Pratt.

A board of trustees holds the title and securities of the association, makes investments, serves in an advisory capacity and meets annually. Members of the board of trustees are E. M. Barnes, Eric Brown, A. B. Connable, Sr., Mrs. Dorothy Dalton, Dr. J. P. Everett, Mrs. Robert Huston, Earl C. Mitchell, Stanley Morris, Charles Pratt, the Rev. B. A. Roberson, Mrs. J. T. Small, William Shakespeare, Jr., Emery Sheppard, Winship Todd, Mrs. L. N. Upjohn, Walter Ware, the Rev. Bernis Warfield, Henry Williams and Mrs. L. H. Woods.

Lee R. Pettiford is executive director of Douglass Community Center. He holds a BS degree from Wilberforce University school of social administration. Prior to accepting a position with the Center, he was group worker at Parkway Community Center, Chicago. Other staff members are Frederick Jefferson, recreation director, who holds a BS degree in physical education from West Virginia State College; Juanita Overby, girls' worker, a graduate of Western Michigan College physical education department; Joyce Jefferson, office secretary, a graduate of Parsons Business school; and Janice Alexander, group worker and librarian, a graduate of Oberlin College.

A program of organized physical activities including basketball for junior and senior boys and girls, physical fitness classes, organized games for children, volley ball, and badminton, is in operation at the Center.

Group activities form an important part of the Center's program. They include Boy and Girl Scout groups, arts and crafts classes, Club 400 for teen-agers, cooking classes, social recreation periods, boys' athletic club, the Fairies club for young girls, Junior Boys' Citizenship club, Hobby club, Co-ed club, and golf, tennis and archery classes.

Operating simultaneously with the organized activities is a special program offering opportunity for free activities such as ping pong, billiards, checkers, dominoes, cards and darts.

For adults there are dramatics, bridge, canasta and pinochle. Among other social and community activities are dances, dinners and teas.

Miss Elizabeth Purchase is general chairman of the membership drive.

Charles Williams, president • Mary McKellar, vice president
Norma Cash, secretary • Alden Byrd, treasurer
Sallie Graine • Elizabeth Purchase
Alma Powell • Edith Williams
Dr. D.V. Estill • Robert Sutton Jr.
Walter Ware • A.B. Connable Jr.
Lawrence Mitchell • Clio Van Valkenburg
Charles Pratt

Pictured: (L to R)
Fred Lilly
Lawrence Mitchell
Eloise Mitchell
Elizabeth Purchase
Pauline Byrd Johnson
Lee Roy Pettiford
Walter White
Rev. David H. Harris
Alden Byrd

Instal Staff at Douglass

6-19-13-50

The nominating committee to select a slate of candidates for offices of Douglas Community Association for 1951 was chosen at last night's annual meeting of the association at the center.

Named to the committee were Alwina Williams, Gladys Kline, James Cloman, Fred Lilly and Sally Graine. This committee will present its slate of candidates for next year's election.

Annual reports were presented by the association's board of directors, finance committee, personnel committee, ways and means committee and Christmas committee. Officers of the association elected last week were installed.

Trustees met annually as advisors to oversee the investments and securities of the organization. These advisors included:

E.M. Barnes • Eric Brown • A.B. Connable Sr.
Dorothy Dalton • Dr. J.P. Everett • Mrs. Robert Huston
Earl C. Mitchell • Stanley Morris • Charles Pratt
The Rev. B.A. Roberson • Mrs. J.T. Small
William Shakespeare Jr. • Emery Sheppard • Winship Todd
Mrs. L.N. Upjohn • Walter Ware • The Rev. Bernis Warfield
Henry Williams • Mrs. L.H. Woods

Color-free Zone

James C. Jackson was president of the Douglass board in 1952 when he praised the Douglass for all it had done in his life. His first memories of the Center were of his six-year-old self being led into the Douglass to take part in activities with others his age. Those who worked there continued to be role models as he matured and went off to serve in the Navy during World War II. Upon his return, he reconnected with the place that he said was "meeting the needs of the individuals in the community irrespective of race or national origin" (*Kalamazoo Gazette*, September 24, 1952).

Jackson's insights were correct: the Douglass did provide a "color-free" zone. However, the comfort Blacks felt there came more out of a lack of opportunity to be accepted at predominantly White recreation facilities. Veterans who fought for their country in World War II returned to a land where a dark cloud of racism seemed to loom over their hopes and dreams.

In Kalamazoo (as in most of the country during the 1940s), the tension and frustration around racism were becoming more intolerable. The first Great Migration of Blacks leaving the South (1910-1940) offered distance from Jim Crow laws and physical hostilities toward Blacks. The Second Great Migration of 1940-1970 was composed of Blacks who sought more economic opportunities and led to a study by Samuel Simmons of Western Michigan University.

He recruited Blacks and Whites to test the culture of businesses based on how the volunteers were served and treated. During an oral history interview of past Douglass employees conducted for the Kalamazoo Valley Museum, Juanita (Overby) Goodwin recalled the study conducted in the 1940s. She said Simmons sent a White couple and a

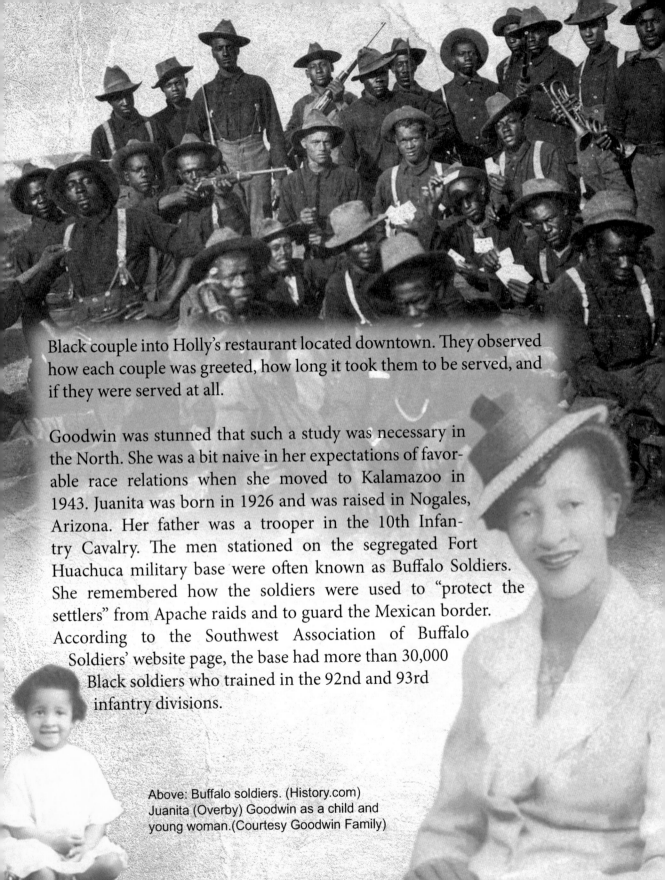

Black couple into Holly's restaurant located downtown. They observed how each couple was greeted, how long it took them to be served, and if they were served at all.

Goodwin was stunned that such a study was necessary in the North. She was a bit naive in her expectations of favorable race relations when she moved to Kalamazoo in 1943. Juanita was born in 1926 and was raised in Nogales, Arizona. Her father was a trooper in the 10th Infantry Cavalry. The men stationed on the segregated Fort Huachuca military base were often known as Buffalo Soldiers. She remembered how the soldiers were used to "protect the settlers" from Apache raids and to guard the Mexican border. According to the Southwest Association of Buffalo Soldiers' website page, the base had more than 30,000 Black soldiers who trained in the 92nd and 93rd infantry divisions.

Above: Buffalo soldiers. (History.com)
Juanita (Overby) Goodwin as a child and young woman.(Courtesy Goodwin Family)

Camp Huachuca provided schools and recreation for the families. It was there that her father taught his three children to play various sports.

Juanita learned to be a fierce competitor in everything from softball to track. However, that family-like community dissolved when soldiers were sent to battle in World War II, leaving the fort nearly deserted. Her father retired but reenlisted only to learn he no longer qualified for family housing. While her brother joined the military, Juanita had one more year of high school to complete.

Not ready to attend the local schools outside the base, she asked if she could finish her senior year one hundred miles away in Phoenix, where her aunt lived. Her parents agreed. By the time she graduated from high school in 1943, her mother had moved to Kalamazoo where another aunt had relocated. Her mother earned extra money by renting a room to Black female Western Michigan University students who were denied the opportunity to live in the dormitories on campus.

The college girls were eager to entertain the young Goodwin and took her downtown for lunch. When they arrived at Holly's restaurant, her appetite was soon spoiled. As they entered the diner, Goodwin saw White patrons seated and eating their meals. The waitress approached them and asked, "How many in your party?" They replied. However, the waitress left without any intention of seating them.

She soon learned that racism in the North wasn't (typically) coupled with verbal backlash or violence. The "rules" that came with denied membership to places like the YMCA, local bowling teams, and university housing provided somewhat diplomatic segregation. Regardless of the scientific studies being conducted to identify racism, it was the Douglass, she would learn, that opened its arms to all, regardless of race or economic status.

A Community's Center

The Community Chest (now United Way) took notice of the organization. Each year, as its staff reviewed grantees, the Douglass was one it was proud to support. The Community Chest named the Douglass one of its Red Feather organizations and granted thousands of dollars annually so the organization could continue to work as an integral force for the enhancement of people of color. What was the secret of this place where White and Colored residents invested and felt they belonged? According to Pettiford, it was an emphasis on leadership through group activities.

"Our work philosophy places emphasis on small interest groups. This allows for more personality interaction and understanding between leader and participant, a really vital factor in the success of our work" (*Kalamazoo Gazette*, September 19, 1951).

Pettiford believed that everyone who took part in activities at the Douglass had a role in its programming, particularly its youth. Students had a wide variety of interests and the Douglass youth leaders did everything to accommodate their quest for knowledge and adventure. An ornithology club was formed to study birds, and painting and sketching clubs brought out the creative side of learning. Teens, in particular, were included in decisions on potential activities through a youth council.

What may have been the secret to fulfilling Pettiford's goals were the educated staff hired to work with youth. His skeleton crew of a secretary, librarian, and custodian had to wear several hats. But he needed young adults with energy and creativity to lead more diverse activities. In 1948 he decided to hire a new Girls' director.

Goodwin had just graduated from WMU. She entered college with a plan to take business courses. However, when she met a student majoring in physical education (who would be "paid to teach kids how to play sports" — which she loved), she asked, "Where do I go to change my curriculum?"

Phyllis (Ashe) Seabolt also attended WMU and was a student role model to Goodwin and other students. While Seabolt also faced discrimination, she broke the glass ceiling. In 1947 she was hired as the first Black secondary teacher for Kalamazoo Public Schools at South Junior High. Her hiring would come just months after that of the first Black teacher in KPS, Pauline Johnson.

Goodwin wouldn't have that opportunity. By the time of her graduation, KPS already employed two Black teachers, and for the administration that was enough. Without any leads or help from her counselor, she learned of the position at the Douglass. She had indeed impressed the board with her fresh ideas and youthful exuberance, but the experience was bitter-sweet. After she was notified of her acceptance, one of the interviewers smugly approached her with a statement she remembered for decades to come.

"She told me that she voted against me. I was in shock!" Goodwin remembered. "I was 21, and that was young. I was raised never to talk back to my elders, but I told that woman, 'Well, somebody had to hire your daughter.'" The woman of the 'no' vote was Edith Belle Hill, whose father Forrest was one of the men who conceptualized the Douglass Center back in 1919. She also was the mother of Pauline Byrd Johnson

Phyllis Ashe Seabolt

who endured tumultuous feelings of bias and prejudice while a student at Kalamazoo College.

In spite of racial apathy, Pauline Byrd Johnson graduated from Kalamazoo College in 1926 as the school's first Black female graduate. She had to seek employment as a teacher in schools from Cass County to Louisville, Kentucky, before she returned to Kalamazoo. Eventually, she was hired to teach at Lincoln Elementary School in 1947, the first Black teacher hired in the local school system. So the comment by Edith Belle Hill to the young Goodwin was surprising, to say the least.

"I was delighted (about the job) and this lady brought me down to despair in a way that it made me not too sure I could *do* the job," Goodwin said.

But Goodwin proved worthy of the position. While she had no idea what to do with the women or youth on their first day together, she challenged them to come up with ideal activities that she would facilitate.

A quartet performs for a women's luncheon. (Douglass Community Association Archives)

FRONT
HORACE COLEMAN
AL TABORN
AL GOODWIN

BACK
SETH FINLEY

PAUL BROWN

Exposing

The concept was successful, and more than one hundred students a day poured into the Douglass to take part in club activities.

She started an integrated Girl Scout troop, taught dance classes, and took students on trips locally and as far as Niagara Falls in Ontario, Canada, to expose them to cultural activities they couldn't get anywhere else. She served as a bridge for race relations with youth through organized sporting events with other centers such as the YMCA, Eastside, and Parchment. In addition, she met her future husband, Robert Goodwin. The two had a whirlwind romance and were wed on July 19, 1950, at Allen Chapel A.M.E. Church.

Youth to the Arts

While Goodwin worked with the girls, Dr. Walden Baskerville was hired as the Boys' director in 1951. His basketball teams earned trophies and bragging rights in contests with teams as far away as Benton Harbor, Michigan. In addition to athletics, he was challenged to enhance the arts as director of Douglass-produced plays. One of his favorites was Tchaikovsky's The Nutcracker.

"This was quite a departure from the annual traditional Christmas program," Baskerville was quoted in the 1984 Douglass Souvenir Booklet. "I was told "they" were not ready for this kind of production, or, it could not be done. But with a large cast of children and adult participation, we did it! I remember the sheer enchantment and enjoyment reflected on the faces of those in the audience. Even today, when I see (those who were in) The Nutcracker, Arabian Dancer, or the Dance of the Sugar Plum Fairy, we greet with smiles and laughter...they remember, too."

Sports, arts, and culture were the focus for daily programming at the Douglass from the 1940s-70s. (Douglass Community Association Archives)

Baskerville left in 1954 for an out-of-state teaching position and the search for a new Boys' director was on. During blizzard-like conditions on February 18, 1956, the board of the Douglass awaited their interview candidate. A young man named John Caldwell was scheduled to interview for the job. He had come with an impressive resume and recommended by the National Recreation Association.

Caldwell was a graduate of Kansas State University who had worked for an extermination company for two years while sending out dozens of resumes across the country. He also worked as a director at a Manhattan, Kansas, recreation center affiliated with the National Recreation Association. Edward Attwell, director of the NRA, felt Caldwell would be the perfect candidate for the position in Kalamazoo.

An educator at heart, Caldwell was eager for an opportunity to leave Kansas and eventually secure a teaching position. If he was hired at the Douglass he would be that much closer to his goal. He drove his 1940 Plymouth from Kansas to Chicago where he stayed the night with extended family. If he wasn't offered the job in Kalamazoo, he planned to return to Chicago, secure a job, and marry his fiancee.

The next day he arrived in a snow-covered Kalamazoo for his 10 a.m. interview. He arrived early with plenty of time to rent a room at the YMCA. After settling in, he drove a few blocks to 231 Ransom Street for the meeting.

"When I arrived everyone (on the interview panel) had left. My watch was set for Chicago time which was an hour behind Kalamazoo time. I was an hour late for the interview," Caldwell remembers.

Teenagers helped drive the activities at the Douglass in the early years.
(Douglass Community Association Archives)

Pettiford and secretary (Corkey) were the only people in the office. Despite the time difference confusion, Pettiford conducted the interview and offered Caldwell the job on the spot. The news of his new job put his marriage plans in motion. On May 26, 1956, Caldwell and his wife, a nurse, were married and made their home in Kalamazoo.

His job hours at the Douglass were from 12:30 - 9:30 p.m., a time most critical to keeping boys occupied with recreation. In the mornings, Caldwell worked at a downtown shoe repair shop, a skill he had learned in Kansas. He would later be hired as a substitute teacher for Kalamazoo Public Schools, one step closer to his goal to teach.

Caldwell immediately met with local ministers to introduce himself and encourage future collaborations. He realized that unlike teaching, where one had a captive audience, a community center needed to provide opportunities that would attract attendees. By 1956, more than 50,000 people came through the doors of the Douglass to participate in its clubs, summer camps, dances, and other internal or partner-hosted activities.

The Don Ami Club was host of the 38th-anniversary tea at the Center. The club was organized in 1930 with the help of charter members Mrs. Michael Johnson and Elsie Warfield. Arthur Washington of the Family Service Center presented the keynote address on the topic of the role of parents.

Downtown Kalamzoo Mall, South Budick Street, 1955. (Kalamazoo County MIGenWeb)

The community depended on the Douglass, and the Douglass depended on the Community Chest. In 1957, a total of $25,000 of its annual budget of $31,667 was provided by the agency. The dependency on the Community Chest, while beneficial, soon would come with challenges.

Kalamazoo Gazette
(Kalamazoo Public Library)

Community Chest Sets $256,872 Goal in Annual Campaign

Kick-off Dinner to Be Held at YMCA for Workers in Local Solicitation.

10-8-50

What you give makes the difference!

Beginning tomorrow that slogan will be the by-word for 431 volunteer workers who will open the 26th annual Community Chest campaign.

Officially, the drive will begin with a kick-off dinner for all workers to be served at 6:30 tomorrow in the YWCA. Tuesday the solicitations will be in full swing with workers aiming their sights at reaching the 1950 goal of $256,872 by the final day of the campaign on Oct. 18.

Dr. T. Thomas Wylie, pastor of the First Baptist church, will be principal speaker at the dinner meeting. The dinner costs are being paid by the Upjohn Company. This is one of the free services of local business and industry through which the Chest campaign expenses are kept to a low of only 2.6 per cent of the goal.

20 AGENCIES BENEFIT

The kick-off dinner will be opened by Cameron L. Davis, president of the Community Chest board of directors. He will later turn the meeting over to J. Bernard Vanderberg, this year's general campaign chairman.

Dinner entertainment will be provided by John Hramie of Western Michigan College and five Western students. George Williams will lead community singing with Mrs. Williams as accompanist.

A total of 20 Red Feather agencies will benefit from funds received in the Chest drive. The campaign is broken down into nine soliciting divisions.

Last year the campaign raised a total of $239,885, making this year's goal 9 per cent higher than the amount subscribed in 1949. The increases, pro-rated among the various divisions, are due principally to installation of a budget item for anticipated expenses stemming from the re-armament program. Chest directors, for example, expect demands from servicemen's organizations before a new fiscal year ends.

DIVISION GOALS

Goals by the various divisions are:

Advance gifts, $139,500; industrial, $39,700; commercial, $2,600; public service, $8,500; professional, $9,200; educational, $9,; governmental, $3,600; men's general, $13,493; women's general, $12,879.

Directing the various divisions are:

Garrett Van Haaften and ___ert E. Scott, advance gifts; ___mund J. Aray, industrial; O. ___ Burdette, commercial; Robert H. Powell, public service; Mrs. H. Colin Hackney and Mrs. Homer

Community Chest, Red Cross '57 Allocations

KCF 0-23-56

AGENCY	1956 Approp.	1957 Tentative Approp.	Dollar Increase	% of 1956
1. Boy Scouts	$ 31,000	$ 34,500	$ 3,500	11.3
2. Child Guidance Clinic	12,500	14,000	1,500	12.0
3. Civic League Home	6,700	5,930	(770)	(11.5)
4. Council of Social Agencies	14,426	14,714	288	1.9
5. Douglas Community Assn.	24,158	25,000	842	3.5
6. Family Service Center	43,000	46,000	3,000	6.9
7. Girl Scouts	17,300	18,300	1,000	5.7
8. Legal Aid Bureau	8,300	8,500	200	2.4
9. Mich. Children's Aid Soc.	25,152	26,000	848	3.4
10. Heege Community Center	20,855	22,500	1,645	7.8
11. Oakwood Youth, Inc.	1,700	1,288	(412)	(24.2)
12. St. Agnes Found. Home	17,000	19,000	2,000	11.7
13. Salvation Army	15,000	17,000	2,000	13.3
14. Student Canteen	1,500	1,500	—2,000	
15. Visting Nurse Assn.	17,300	19,000	1,700	9.8
16. What-So-Ever Free Bed				
17. Y.M.C.A.	900	900		
18. Y.W.C.A.	34,000	38,000	4,000	11.7
19. Chest Office	36,000	40,000	4,000	11.1
20. Chest Campaign	16,515	16,803	288	1.7
21. Shrinkage	11,625	12,145	520	4.4
Totals	363,431	390,080		
22. Constance Brown Society	8,500	9,000	500	5.8
23. Assn. for Ret. Children	—	26,649		7.3
Totals	363,431	407,396	3,818	
24. Reserve Account (2%)	7,196	13,498	13,498	
Totals	370,627	415,544	43,965	12.1
25. American Red Cross	94,132	101,036	44,917	13.2
GRAND TOTALS	$464,759	$516,580	6,904	12.1
			$51,821	7.3
				11.1

"For what now seems like the long ago and almost forgotten past, I served several years on the Board of the Douglass Community Association and one year I had the honor and pleasure of serving as president. This was during the reign of the dependable and affable Lee Pettiford. I recall nothing dramatic or earth-shaking which occurred, but we wrestled with the usual salaries and vacation time and budgetary constraints. All in all, it was a rewarding and happy experience."

Judge Clark M. Olmsted

"Why would they hire someone so dark?"

Changing Tide

1960

Table tennis and pool were common recreational activities played in the lower level of the Douglass. However, Juanita Goodwin had loved sports her entire life and the diversity of her talents never ceased to amaze the youth and adults. She was a city champion in table tennis and could play basketball as well as any of the young men. Caldwell enjoyed tennis, but like the youth of the Douglass, he would be introduced to a game not many in the Black community played—golf. Goodwin was a local women's golf champion who introduced the sport to a new generation.

She created a makeshift golf course in the gym by cutting a hole in the middle of triple-layered carpet squares. The golf "holes" were stationed around the gym for students to attempt to sink the Wiffle balls into. Those who may have never held a golf club learned the correct way to position themselves for a successful swing. In addition, she shared the rules of the game, how to record scores, and simple course etiquette.

JOHN CALDWELL

Caldwell Is Douglass President

KG 8-2-68

John Caldwell, assistant principal at Central High School, was named president of the Douglass Community Association Board of Directors Thursday.

Other officers elected at the board meeting at the agency were Dr. Lewis Walker, vice president; Gene Moon, treasurer; and Robert Travis, secretary.

James S. Gilmore and Charles O'Neal were elected to the executive committee, to serve at-large with the officers of the board.

Committee chairman appointed were Dr. Walker, personnel and program; Moon, finance; Probate Judge John Pikaart, legislation and by-laws; and Mrs. Clifford Whitten, public relations.

Caldwell also named the following members to represent DCA on the following boards: Wyatt D. Kirk, Rev. B. Moses James and Mrs. Clifford Whitten, Interfaith Housing Council; Kirk, Greater Kalamazoo Council; and Al Taborn, Kal-Cap.

The board's regular meeting date was set for 8 p.m. the second Thursday of each month.

Douglass Purpose Changed

Oct 5 6 62

A change of purpose for the Douglass Community Association is planned as the outgrowth of a study of neighborhood social problems.

The Community Chest agency will switch from a recreational to an inter-racial neighborhood center working with social problems within the Kalamazoo North Side. .

The change was jointly announced by Robert R. Goodwin, president of the Douglass Community Association, and Neil K. Plantefaber, president of the Kalamazoo Community Chest.

THE STUDY was made by Robert L. Bond, a representative of the National Federation of Settlement, with the cooperation of board members from Douglass and the Community Chest.

In its new role Douglass will work with churches and other organizations, with individuals and families, regardless of religious, racial or economic conditions within the area.

Work will be centered around such functions as helping to develop a "sense of neighborhood within the community" and helping where possible to strengthen family life "by guiding parents and children to a clearer understanding of each other."

DOUGLASS DIRECTOR Lee R. Pettiford says work will be directed also toward individuals to develop "their fullest capacities, and to strengthen relationships between neighbors within the community."

Adds Pettiford, "The job is a big one, and will take time to accomplish. Through the support of the community, it can be accomplished."

More than Recreation

The war era provided a home for soldiers and youth programming helped mold good citizens. Now, Director Lee Pettiford felt it was time for a shift. Caldwell and Goodwin used recreation to teach the youth skills such as teamwork, leadership, conflict resolution, and respect—skills that would help them as students and in the workforce. Pettiford had always been outspoken about the need for the entire community to work toward integrated programming, not just the Douglass.

He challenged the board to take bolder steps to push collaborations, but many felt that everything Blacks needed could be provided by the Douglass. He wanted to broaden its scope to take on neighborhood issues and strengthen individuals, moving away from being seen only for recreational purposes.

City May Take Over Douglass Recreation

The city will take over the recreation program of Douglass Community Association if the Recreation Commission approves such an arrangement.

The City Commission Monday night accepted a recommendation of Com. Arthur Washington Jr. that the recreation activities at the north side establishment be incorporated into the city program for the remainder of this year.

The measure will be presented to the Recreation Commission next week for final approval.

Washington explained that plans are for the association to concentrate more on the "settlement house" type activities rather than recreational functions.

Whether the city will assume responsibility for providing a recreational program at the center on a permanent basis will be determined later by the commission.

In 1959, Arthur Washington, Jr., was elected Kalamazoo's first Black city commissioner. He, too, called for the city to help change the focus of the Douglass from recreation to the "settlement house" model of community change. Washington recommended that the city take on the recreation programs of the Douglass to open the door for more social work-type programs (*Kalamazoo Gazette*, November 6, 1962). A paper published in the Journal of Sociology and Social Welfare (June 2003) by Beverly Koerin stated that settlement houses were seen as the key to social change from the front line. "The twin objectives of the settlement movement were to provide immediate services and to work for social reform."

Therefore, settlement leaders were also involved in social reform activities. They influenced municipal governments to set aside land for parks and playgrounds and to improve sanitation and public health programs; they engaged in political activism to effect reform at local, state, and national levels on such issues as minimum wage, child labor laws, and women's suffrage. Thus, the settlement house movement reflected a dual responsibility for social service and social reform. The "most immediate work" of the settlement was to meet individual needs.

Kalamazoo Gazette (Kalamazoo Public Library)
Local residents wore these buttons to the historic March on Washington. (Douglass Community Center Archives)

The Douglass' reputation was based on its ability to provide mentorship and positive role models to youth, who would go on to contribute to their community. There were always volunteers available to help plan Christmas parties for the youth or help a young mother obtain furniture or clothing for her children. Recreation had been a means to provide a service to the Black community. That method was at risk of becoming obsolete. A new direction—to work outside the walls of the Douglass—was being encouraged and virtually required by the Community Chest.

In response, the leadership of the Douglass proposed a five-point plan:

5 points

- **To strengthen family relations**
- **To develop a sense of neighborhood on the Northside**
- **To help individuals develop to their fullest capabilities**
- **To strengthen ties among different cultural, economic racial, and religious groups**
- **To train citizens in democracy**

This plan seemed to have the stamp of approval from the board, but in February 1963, as the plan was being implemented by Pettiford, Community Chest withdrew their membership and funding to the Douglass.

Douglass Community Association Archives

Katherine Johnson was a mathematician at NASA and was instrumental in the spaceflights.
(Credit: NASA) Below: Focus New Comic.

Taking a Stand

The 1960s were a decade of scientific innovation. The United States celebrated its moon landing in 1969, and over a ten-year period the world would see inventions such as the laser to touch-tone phones, video games, hand-held calculators, and the audio cassette. The world was demanding more and wanted it faster than ever. With that also came an even stronger demand for equal rights for all.

Even those in Kalamazoo were fed up with the Jim Crow segregation mentality of local businesses and the school system. Duane Roberts, a local NAACP president, brought attention to the city regarding the segregated schools. While the South had its historic policies regarding segregated schools, Midwest states also carried some of those same beliefs. In 1955 the U.S. Supreme Court ruled segregated schools were illegal after the case Brown vs. the Board of Education of Topeka, Kansas. However, by the late '60s more than ninety percent of the Black students in the city attended five of the 29 elementary schools, only three of its secondary schools, and most attended Central High as opposed to Loy Norrix High.

Some local businesses and recreation facilities also maintained segregation-based practices. Juanita Goodwin intentionally brought her students from the Douglass to the local skating rink on the night designated for Whites only. When the attendant refused to let them skate and threatened to call the police, she stood her ground. The attendant realized Goodwin was willing to stand up for the youth, regardless of any potential repercussions from the law. Sit-ins were all over the national news and the rink did not need that kind of attention. Goodwin and the students won and were allowed to skate any night they chose.

A block away from the Douglass, on the corner of North and Burdick streets, another storm was brewing. When 17-year-old David Johnson and friend Walter Jones, III., were denied an opportunity to apply for jobs at the drugstore of Donald and Mary Jane Van Avery, it led to action. Their friends Charles Warfield and

Drug Store Picketed By Negroes

Ten Negro pickets today marched in front of Van Avery Drug Store at 702 N. Burdick, protesting what they said was the owner's refusal to consider hiring Negroes.

City Community Relations Director Richard Anderson met late this morning with representatives of the drug store and the local branch of the National Association for the Advancement of Colored People, which threw up the picket line.

No agreement was reached, and the meeting broke up about 11:30.

Kalamazoo police said the pickets were orderly.

NAACP Branch President Mrs. Amerriel Overton said she and the Rev. Donald Holt, minister of the North Presbyterian Church, attempted to meet with drug store owner Donald W. Van Avery last week but were rebuffed."

Mrs. Overton said the group had received two complaints from two young Negro high

(Kalamazoo Central High School Yearbooks Online)
News articles courtesy of Alma Jones collection.

Malcolm Earhart were motivated by the recent events in the South that showed violence toward Blacks who bucked against Jim Crow segregation policies. The young men worked with the local NAACP to organize a local boycott that began on June 17, 1963.

The Northside neighborhood had gas stations, grocery stores, salons, and other businesses owned mainly by Whites. The area had a large population of Dutch before Blacks began to migrate north and into Kalamazoo. While the Van Averys were not the only owners whose policies were not favorable toward Blacks, the Van Avery boycott could set the tone for other businesses who practiced discrimination in hiring.

KALAMAZOO GAZETTE

nesday, June 19, 1963. Section 2—Pages 19-36.

CKETING CONTINUES

ope for Possible 'Middle Ground' greement at Van Avery's Reported

cketing continued today at Avery Drug Store, 702 N. dick, as store representatives with local officials of the ional Association for the Ad cement of Colored People ity Hall for two hours this ning.

o settlement had been hed, Community Relations ctor Richard Anderson re ed just before noon, but he "There is still a possibility sides can get together on iddle ground."

The NAACP is asking that e north side drug store hire qualified Negro as either part-time clerk or soda foun in worker and promise to nsider a Negro as a full-time erk when a job opening de lops. All present employes e white.

The NAACP also reportedly omised to refer customers to n Avery's in order to increase siness if the terms were met. Anderson said Mrs. Donald n Avery, wife of the owner, ced to get in touch with her sband, who is out of town, d report the NAACP's posi n.

NAACP is the prime organiz of the bi-racial picket line in nt of the drug store in a 14 ur-a-day basis. The picket e was first put up Monday.

THE DRUG STORE'S position, s. Van Avery told The Ga tte this morning, is that it sn't done anything wrong. Names of two colored persons king work have been taken, hough it's unlikely there will any vacancies, she said. Morever, "any number of ite students" have applied re ntly, she said, but no appli tions were accepted. Thus, egroes and whites are being eated equally, Mrs. Van Avery id.

Other stores in the com munity she has contacted operate the same way — re fusing to take applications un less there is work available, she said.

She said one of the young Negroes whose application the store had allegedly refused to

Windows Broken

One small window was broken out with a stone and a larger window cracked Tuesday night in the same block where Van Avery's drug store was being picketed.

Employes at Buck's Bar, 708 N. Burdick, heard the small window broken at about 8:30 p.m. The crack in the large window was discovered at closing time.

No report of the incident was made, according to city police.

take had merely asked her, in an off-hand way while making a purchase, for a job. She said she hadn't thought he was seri ous at the time.

Mrs. Van Avery said a couple

of persons are taken on during the school year but do not work during the summer. And busi ness conditions are such that a college girl who usually works summers was not re-hired this year.

She said her husband's ill ness has restricted his activities and that he never "rebuffed" visitors from the NAACP who wanted to negotiate.

VAN AVERY employes have an average seniority of 13.8 years, and the junior employes, not counting the school year help, have all been there at least 2½ or three years. Mrs. Van Avery said emphatically that none of these would be fired to make room for new comers.

Store Manager Harold Diet rich added that many colored persons have called to say they are in sympathy with the store but are afraid to cross the picket lines. Necessities are being delivered in some cases, Dietrich said.

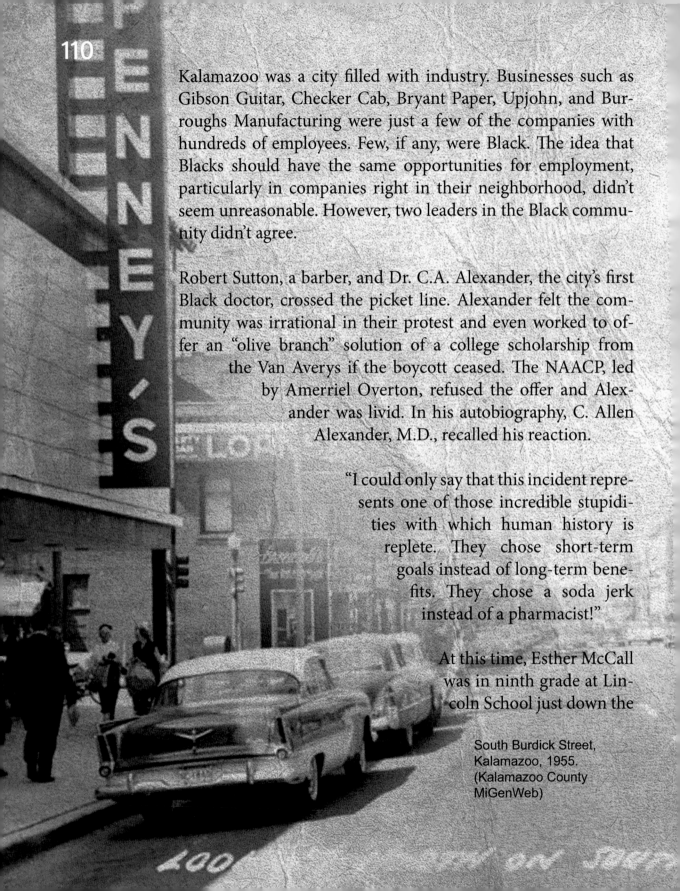

Kalamazoo was a city filled with industry. Businesses such as Gibson Guitar, Checker Cab, Bryant Paper, Upjohn, and Burroughs Manufacturing were just a few of the companies with hundreds of employees. Few, if any, were Black. The idea that Blacks should have the same opportunities for employment, particularly in companies right in their neighborhood, didn't seem unreasonable. However, two leaders in the Black community didn't agree.

Robert Sutton, a barber, and Dr. C.A. Alexander, the city's first Black doctor, crossed the picket line. Alexander felt the community was irrational in their protest and even worked to offer an "olive branch" solution of a college scholarship from the Van Averys if the boycott ceased. The NAACP, led by Amerriel Overton, refused the offer and Alexander was livid. In his autobiography, C. Allen Alexander, M.D., recalled his reaction.

"I could only say that this incident represents one of those incredible stupidities with which human history is replete. They chose short-term goals instead of long-term benefits. They chose a soda jerk instead of a pharmacist!"

At this time, Esther McCall was in ninth grade at Lincoln School just down the

South Burdick Street, Kalamazoo, 1955. (Kalamazoo County MiGenWeb)

block from Van Avery's. Ninety percent of the students were Black and frequented the store often. One day, her counselor called her to the office with a proposition to consider being the first Black hired at the drug store. She was told to think about it and ask her parents. They agreed and felt this would be an opportunity for their often shy daughter to do something to benefit not only herself but her community.

The six-week boycott ended with the hiring of McCall. To her, it was a job, but her counselor expressed it would mean more than just a paycheck.

For the community, they won through their organized, nonviolent stance.

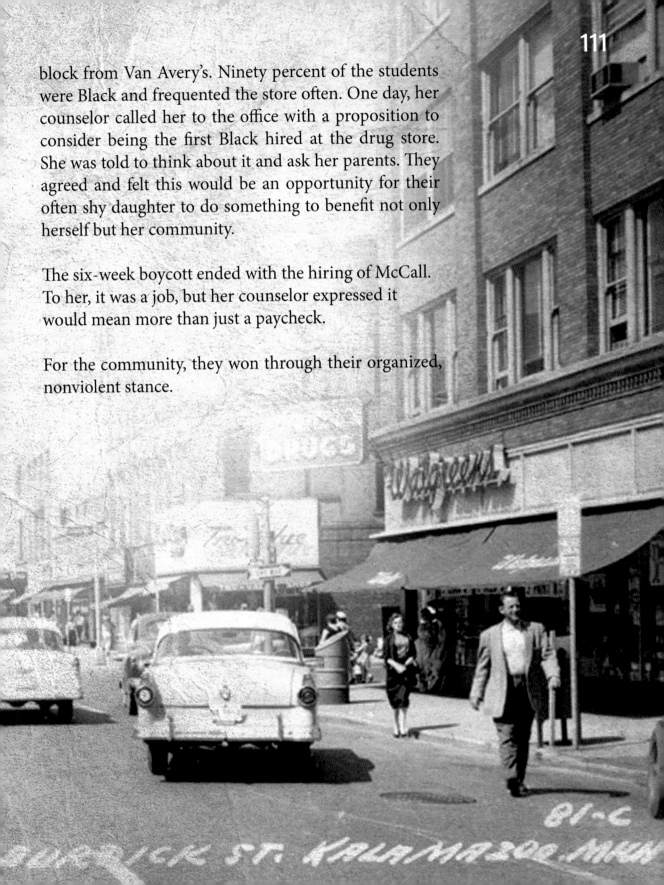

"At the time I thought, this would be my little moment to shine, or to make a change in my community. I felt honored that I would be asked among other children...they picked out qualities in me that would work in that kind of situation. They felt that maybe I would fit in maybe a little better and I think that had a lot to do with it." (Kalamazoo Valley Museum interview, 2009)

She was welcomed by the Van Averys and staff who appreciated her respectful manners and good work ethic. At first, she only worked during her school lunch hour behind the scenes, to help prepare the lunches. In the summer, she was out front more and felt the prejudice of White customers who didn't appreciate her presence. A year after McCall's hiring, the owners changed their policies to hiring more minorities. One of those girls had a darker skin tone than McCall and one of the White workers said, "Why would they hire someone so dark?" To that McCall answered, "Because of her abilities, not because of the color of her skin."

The Van Averys eventually sold their store. Other businesses on the Northside would also be targeted for not hiring Blacks, and Arthur Washington, the first Black city commissioner, used his position as a former commissioner (1959-1969) to meet with company leaders to urge them to hire Blacks. His bold efforts to organize pickets and a march on Kalamazoo City Hall led to companies at least being aware that the Black community did desire work in establishments in their neighborhoods such as Gibson Guitar, according to an interview with Washington by the Kalamazoo Valley Museum (2009).

The community had brought about a change with the help of the local churches, the NAACP, and the Douglass Center. The collaboration of organizations was just what Pettiford envisioned for the Douglass. However, those who held the Community Chest purse strings disagreed with his plan. The board received notice that funds would cease unless they did three things:

1) Increase the board with a wider representation of the community,
2) Shift to the settlement format, and
3) Fire Lee Roy Pettiford!

Pettiford was fired. As promised, by the fall of 1963 funds from the Community Chest had been reinstated as all of their "requests" were fulfilled. With all recreation activities being folded into City recreation programs, Caldwell moved from Boys' director to the Douglass' interim director. Juanita Goodwin left the Center in 1957 to

Douglass Community Association May Lose Chest Agency Support

K/ 5-21-63

The Douglass Community Association, for years the focal point of Negro activities in Kalamazoo, today faces the most difficult problem in its 44-year history.

Caught in the web of a shifting population on the city's North Side, a low economic status among those it tries to serve, a squeeze on charitable funds and a confused picture of just what its community mission should be, the Douglass Community Association would seem to be in real trouble.

The Community Chest of Kalamazoo County, of which Douglass is a charter member has expressed its dissatisfaction with the Douglass program by notifying the association that Community Chest financial support and membership for Douglass will be terminated as of Dec. 31, 1963. The action was taken by the Chest board Feb. 8.

Chest funds in the amount of $25,790 have been provided for this year.

IN CUTTING Douglass from Community Chest support, the Chest board listed several reasons for its move but also left the door open for action by Douglass which might permit its return to Chest membership.

The board of directors of the Chest said, in effect, that if Douglass Community Association, or any other qualified organization can prove that it is willing and able to provide a program which will effectively meet North Side neighborhood needs as outlined in a recent

Douglass Center Restored To Membership in Chest

K/ 6-14-63

The Community Chest of Kalamazoo County has restored Douglass Community Association to the status of participating member of the Chest.

The Community Chest board, which had cut Douglas from Chest membership in February because of "a number of factors and pressures which could no longer be ignored," has informed the north side agency that changes made by the Douglass board since February have met the conditions cited in the severance announcement.

IN THE February letter terminating both Chest membership and financial support as of December of this year, the Chest board listed three major areas of dissatisfaction with the Douglass operations:

1. It was felt that the Douglass board needed enlarging and that wider community representation be reflected in the membership.
2. The shift of Douglass into a settlement house form of community service, recommended by the 1962 Bond survey of the north side, had shown little progress.
3. A lack of confidence in present Douglass staff leadership was evident within the Community Chest board and within important segments of the north side community.

In a statement to the Douglass board issued during the past week, the Community Chest stated that changes in the composition of the Douglass board and administrative staff indicated a desire to follow the recommendations of the Chest and of the Bond survey. The changes had included the enlarging of the Douglass board, the termination of the services of Lee Roy Pettiford as Douglass director and the adoption of a tentative program of service to new residents of the north side; a girls' program; plans for a Golden Agers group; a farm and garden camp and assistance to ADC (Aid To Dependent Children) mothers in the area.

THE COMMUNITY Chest and Douglass boards are to form a joint committee to study financial and service programs for Douglass for the remainder of 1963 and for 1964.

The Douglass Community Association will hold its annual meeting and election of board members and officers at 8 Wednesday evening, June 12, at the Douglass Center, 231 E. Ransom.

Lee Pettiford's vision for the Douglass ends when he is fired to appease funders. (Kalamazoo Gazette)

LEE R. PETTIFORD
Community Leader

work as a physical education teacher at South Junior High. Pettiford immediately relocated to Norristown, Pennsylvania, to work as a social worker in a state hospital.

Pettiford served the Douglass as director from 1947 to 1962, longer than any other director thus far. It may have been his ties as a native of Kalamazoo that allowed him to use all of his energy to give back to the community he called home. Future directors would not maintain the longevity needed for consistent growth during the new settlement approach to community change.

Finding a new leader would not only be the task of the Douglass. The country also, would face changes in leadership. On November 22, 1963, President John F. Kennedy was assassinated during a motorcade through the streets of Dallas, Texas, where he planned several political speeches. Lyndon B. Johnson, the vice president, was sworn in as the 36th President of the United States. The country waited to see if Johnson would continue to push the bill Kennedy had proposed to Congress just months earlier, the Civil Rights Bill.

In Search of a Leader

As Caldwell transitioned into his role as director, he brought in new ideas. He implemented a nine-point program for fall activities that included a resource guide of neighborhood churches, social service agencies, and other places in the community. However, his passion was teaching. In the first week of 1964, the board accepted his resignation with respect for his ambitions to work in the Kalamazoo Public Schools. After more than eight years of juggling his duties at the Douglass with substitute teaching, he had a full-time job as a boys' guidance counselor.

His work at the Douglass, and the relationships he had established with the youth and parents, were a benefit to his new position.

In 1964, the Kalamazoo Community Foundation provided a $20,000 grant to the Rev. B. Moses James, board president. The funds would be used toward much-needed renovations on the now nearly 25-year-old building. As the board searched for a new director, it also decided to close the building in the summer through Labor Day for repairs. The newly-acquired farm from Kenneth Melching would serve as a retreat center to host summer camp programs.

Heading North, He Donates Farm

Kenneth Melching Gives 40-Acre Homestead to Douglass Center

By ALLEN T. CONN, Gazette Staff Writer

A gentle, lonely man, whose greatest pleasure is looking into the smiling face of a small child, has made a gift of all his wordly possessions so that a great number of children can be made happy for years to come.

Kenneth Melching, a 51-year-old farmer with a Quaker background who has spent most of his life as a sea-faring globe-trotter, left Kalamazoo last week carrying only a suitcase. He left behind a 40-acre farm at 9th street and Hart drive, northwest of Kalamazoo, which he had just deeded to the Douglass Community Center.

He made no restrictions on the outright gift, asking only that the land, buildings and livestock be utilized to provide happiness for the greatest number of children possible. The Negro community center plans to let other organizations share in the benefits.

Melching has no children. He was married several years ago, but is now divorced. His only relatives are a brother, L. W. Melching of 1012 Mills, and a sister, Mrs. Elmer Butler, living south of Oshtemo on 4th street.

Before leaving Wednesday, Melching had lunch with the Rev. Alfred Halsted, pastor of Sunnyside Methodist Church and treasurer of the Douglass center.

CALLING HIMSELF an incurable nomad, Melching told the Rev. Halsted that he wanted to head north into Canada while he still has his health, to homestead a place and stake a claim up there.

He said he wanted to return to an isolated spot he'd found on one of his trips — miles away from the nearest post office and rail head.

"All I know is, it's located somewhere north of the Straits," the Rev. Halsted said. He wanted to get up there while there was still snow on the ground so he could watch the spring run-off and pick a good drainage area.

Like another southwestern Michigan farmer before him, Melching's interest in farming had been waning because of what he had called senseless government restrictions, regulations and questionnaires. Stanley Yankus of Dowagiac, who revolted against government controls, left a year ago for Australia after selling his farm.

A donation by Kenneth Melching in 1960 provided new opportunities for the organization. He had admired the work the Center did for the youth, so upon relocating to Canada he donated forty acres of farmland. For decades, youth workers, parents, and other volunteers carpooled dozens of youth to lakes and parks throughout West Michigan for swimming, fishing, and camping. Melching's donation of prime farmland on Ninth Street and Hart Drive offered a new place for families and groups to plant vegetables, have a picnic, or just enjoy nature.

40 Acres Farmland Donated

Executive Director Appointed by Douglass Community Center Board

KG 7/5/64

By July, the board approved the hire of Reginald Gary who had worked in Battle Creek. His resume was impressive, and the 38-year-old husband and father of two seemed a good fit for an organization focused on the family. He had a bachelor of arts degree and a master's degree from Atlanta University, where he had met his wife, who was a nurse. Gary came on board with a dedication to the new settlement model that impressed Community Chest. The funders voted to provide $35,000 toward the Douglass that included hiring two new outreach workers. But the honeymoon lasted less than a year as Gary resigned, leaving the center for a similar position in Syracuse, New York.

In a farewell letter published in the Kalamazoo Gazette, Gary shared the challenges the community would face if it didn't work together to help those of all races and income levels.

"Kalamazoo is growing, its industry is expanding and changing character. Along with industrial progress, you will also get the problem of low-income groups who will need adequate housing and job training and won't be able to provide these for themselves. They will be both Negro and white. They will increase as Kalamazoo grows. You won't be able to ignore them."

New York City received national attention in 1965 with the assassination of Malcolm X. Born Malcolm Little and raised in Lansing, Michigan, the former Nation of Islam

Above: The Douglass replaces Pettiford with Reginald Gary who would soon be replaced by James Horn (next page). Right: Malcomb X was assassination in 1965 as the Civil Rights Era was underway. (Kalamazoo Gazette)

KG 9-5-65

By JAMES STOMMEN
Gazette Staff Writer

minister and spokesperson was killed during a speech in the Audubon Ballroom on February 21st. He was 39 years old.

As the news of Malcolm X's death settled, Kalamazoo searched for yet another director to lead the Douglass. This time, James Horn, a Grand Rapids native with educational and professional ties to the University of Michigan, made the "team." Horn had an athletic background in baseball and football. He had once played for the Kansas City Monarchs and had a master's degree in social work from the University of Michigan. Although he had hop-scotched to jobs in Illinois, Michigan, and New York, he seemed dedicated to working at the Douglass and being closer to his family in Grand Rapids. His children were enrolled at Western Michigan University's High and Campus schools (elementary and junior high).

Horn brought a three-pronged program to the Douglass and the possibility of funds from the Office of Economic Opportunity's "war on poverty" purse. In addition, Community Chest provided thousands toward an intake center housed in the organization. They would focus on five census tracts (neighborhoods): approximately 1,070 families who were identified as living in poverty. According to reports by Horn, the Northside had twenty-five percent of the 5,000 people in the county reported to be living in poverty. Comstock had the second-highest number of poor.

The approach, dubbed IntReFol would include:

Intake: Locating families and problems and helping identify their difficulties,

Referral: Determining what local agencies could be used as referrals, and

Follow-Up: Helping clients use existing services.

"We want to help people reach their goals," said Horn in the article "Douglass Plan to Enlarge Services Receives Backing." He added, "As social workers, we don't do things FOR people, rather we do things with them...our basic purpose is to move people into the mainstream of life in Kalamazoo" (*Kalamazoo Gazette*, September 26, 1966).

COMING ON STRONG!

ONE GIFT WORKS MANY WONDERS

With your fair share support, the 60 Kalamazoo County Community Chest agencies can continue their job of helping people. Part of the $1,176,589 Chest campaign goal will go this year to help support work at

Douglass Community Association

The "Intrefol" program of Douglass Community Association is attempting to provide assistance to individuals and families with "multi-problems." Elements of "Intrefol" include outreach to make contact with persons needing help; evaluation of goals and resources (education, employment, health); of the individuals or families; referral to community resources; assistance in contacting and communicating with other agencies; and follow-up to ensure action being taken. Here Al Lang, director of Michigan Migrant Opportunities, Region III confers with Douglass director, James Horn.
—Gazette photo

The organization received more than $50,000 in local and federal funding needed to hire the staff to carry out the IntReFol mission. Shirley Lowman was hired as the full-time director of the program and the first full-time White employee at the Center. She supervised ten other new staff hired and stationed at 231 Ransom Street.

As community leaders watched, the Douglass was seen as an organization that could advocate for racial harmony. The IntReFol mission would be the key, but in a different way. What started in 1919 as an organization specifically to provide a service to Colored soldiers in

Douglass Will Administer Intrefol Poverty Program

need of social, recreational, and moral support now promoted integration. In addition, the funds provided by the federal government for IntReFol came with a national philosophy the organization had to adopt to remain compliant.

The board agreed with the new direction. At the same time, they called on local leaders to work to address housing. They drafted a resolution to the City Commission to form a Housing Commission. Board members included: Wyatt Kirk, president; Dwight King, vice president; Mrs. Harold DePree, secretary; Dr. Hugh V. Anderson, treasurer.

The National Federation of Settlements and Neighborhood Centers adopted a statement that all who took part and received funds for settlement programs would abide by. Portions of the bold statement denounced any participation with militant groups, civil disobedience, and violence.

"We understand the need for excluded minority groups to band together for self-help and mutual aid. But we believe that settlements must press for a society in which differences are not the basis for exclusion or special privilege but are cherished as part of the vast human mosaic. The federation believes that individuals and groups can and must confront one another—not to destroy—but to build a more perfect nation.

'Intrefol' Program Douglass Enlarged

"Therefore we believe settlements and neighborhood centers are best comprised of people who have vital and deep roots in the neighborhood, together with people of the wider community who have a concern for the neighborhood and its importance and who can translate neighborhood needs to the larger community" ("Guidelines Adopted by Douglass," *Kalamazoo Gazette*, December 27, 1967).

Again, those holding the purse strings seemed to control the direction of the Douglass. In the meantime, the organization focused on IntReFol efforts, and employment for residents was the main concern. With the various corporations in the county, the Douglass would connect to learn of job openings and opportunities the companies could provide for their clients. Earlier that year, efforts were made to help those who found jobs secure their earnings. The Douglass opened its very own North Community Credit Union.

The local *Focus* newspaper reported in its February 1967 edition that the "Credit Union Was the First of its Kind in the State." George Wade was the credit union's president and urged those in Census Tracts 1-10 (North and East side residents) to become members and support with at least 50 cents to $1 in deposits each week. Some of the charter members of the organization included Mabel Irvine, Connie Reese, and Ray Clark. Officers included Mary Morris, vice president; Harold Mason, treasurer; and the Rev. Bernis Warfield, Jr., Carol Davis, and Barbara Mion as board members. The credit union was open from 1-4 p.m. Mondays, Wednesdays, and Fridays.

FOCUS

Kalamazoo, Michigan

FEBRUARY, 1967

N ORTH E AST WS

VOL. II, No. 9   *"Presenting a Community in Action"*

CREDIT UNION READY FOR BUSINESS

With a few gulps at the seriousness of it all and a "heave ho" the North Community Credit Union got under-way at its first annual meeting January 18 at the Douglass Community Center with 31 persons attending.

It brought to a cul-mination months of hard work, gatherings and a general "meeting of minds" of various ele-ments in the community to determine how it should get off the ground.

The North Community Credit Union is the first of its kind in Michigan. Its member-ship is based upon the common bond of living or working in Census Tracts Numbers 1 through 5. This en-compasses generally the north, northwest, and northeast are—of the city about ~

The Long Dry Summer

HISTORY OF NEGRO IN LIMELIGHT

The Women's Auxiliary of the Douglass Commun-ity Association will sponsor their second annual observance of National Negro History Week with a program at Douglass February 12 at 4 p.m.

Powell Lindsay, pres-ident of The Research Association for Michi-gan Negro History, Inc., Lansing, will be the keynote speaker, speak-ing on "The Negro's Lost Legacy".

Art and literature exhibits of both the Negro American and Af-rican Negro will be on display. Also, several

(Cont. on p.2)

"Negro History as Unit Not Taught"

"Negro history as a unit in itself is not taught at Lincoln," said Jack Blanke, pr——al of the elementary school, when querried if Ne-gro histo——   —taught the pupils.

H—   ———at the library there has many books with Negro
———, in the teaching of citizenship and social
———the subject is taught. In explaining how this
———following ways—through pictures in the hall,
———ing Brotherhood Week) and teachers hired that
———udents' needs."

———ipal at Roosevelt Elementary school, said
———e general principles in their school.

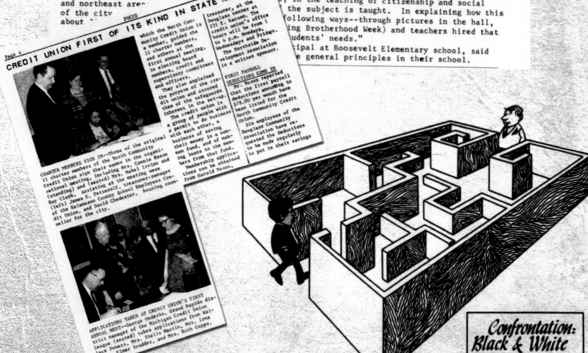

CREDIT UNION FIRST OF ITS KIND IN STATE

CHARTER MEMBERS SIGN IN—Three of the original 11 charter members of the North Community Credit Union sign their names in the organi-zational meeting, including Mrs. Connie Reese (standing) and (seated) Mrs. Mabel Irvine and Roy Clark. Assisting at the meeting were (left) James E. Fetterolf, treasurer-manager of the Kalamazoo County School Employees Cre-dit Union, and David Chedester, housing coun-sellor for the city.

which the North Com-munity Credit Union is a member, guides the 11 charter members, and others at the first annual meeting, in electing board members, credit and supervisory committees and officers.

They also explained the purpose of the cre-dit union and assured them the safeguards inherent in the set-up. The credit union is a group of people with a permit to do business with each other, a business of saving their money in a com-mon fund, and of mak-ing loans to the mem-bers from that fund. Membership applica-tions can be obtained from Harold Mason.

treasurer, at the Douglass center at 331 E. Ransom. The credit union's office hours will be from 1 to 4 p.m. Mondays, Wednesdays and Fridays. The Northside De-velopment Association is a written sponsor.

FIRST PAYROLL DEDUCTIONS COME IN

Mr. Mason reported that the first payroll deductions amounting to $75.00 per month have been listed for the North Community Credit Union. Six employees of the Douglass Community Association have re-quested the deductions to be made regularly to put in their savings

APPLICATIONS TAKEN AT CREDIT UNION'S FIRST ANNUAL MEET—George Ondeion, Grand Rapids dis-trict manager of the Michigan Credit Union League, (seated) takes applications from Wal-lace Powers, Mrs. Stella Martin, Mrs. Irma Baker, Elmer Scudder, and Mrs. Ruth Copps.

Confrontation:
Black & White

Just as the community worked to better its residents, news of the murder of the Rev. Dr. Martin Luther King, Jr., rocked the nation. On April 4th, 1968, King was gunned down by a sniper while standing on the balcony of the Lorraine Motel in Memphis, Tennessee. He was in Memphis to speak up for the rights of Black sanitation workers who were forced to work in deplorable conditions with little pay.

Those in Kalamazoo also were flooded with emotions. Days after the assassination, John Caldwell was promoted to principal of Kalamazoo Central High School to help manage race riots that occurred in the chaos of enraged students. In addition, students across the country protested the U.S. military draft during the Vietnam War.

Political and race riots shook cities across the country. Local residents who planned to attend King's Poor People's Campaign in Washington, D.C., learned the event scheduled for Memorial Day (1968) had been postponed to June. The organizers of the initiative needed time to grieve and regroup after King's assassination.

In the meantime, Kalamazoo's Black residents continued to seek employment at local companies. However, not two years into the new direction of the Douglass to serve as an employment training and placement agency, the local Fisher Body automobile assembly plant asserted that the Douglass staff had not provided adequate employees in a timely manner. Douglass board president Wyatt Kirk was frustrated when the issue was brought up at a board meeting of their fiduciary agent, the Kalamazoo County Community Action Program (Kal-Cap).

Kirk said the Fisher Body representative should have gone directly to the Douglass with their concerns and not Kal-Cap (*Kalamazoo*

Gazette, May 23, 1968). That complaint maybe have been one reason that led Kal-Cap to cut their $42,000 funding to the Center in half the following year, using the money to start other neighborhood centers.

Tensions were high as the Civil Rights Bill of 1964 (to prevent segregation everywhere from public parks to the workplace) was implemented. Not all employers welcomed the mandate. Community organizers, people who could relate, hear, and provide answers for those in the neighborhoods, were in great demand. Kalamazoo was in need of a community organizer and the Metropolitan Church Council was on the mission to find one. But, just as quickly as they began their search, they learned that a local man with deep roots in the community had just been hired at the Douglass for that same position.

After serving in the military and earning a master's degree in social work from Wayne State University, 27-year-old Moses Walker was the perfect man for the job. His connection with the Douglass was in the brick and mortar. His father had worked on the construction of the building as a Work Progress Administration (WPA) employee back in 1940. Young Walker began his own education in the nursery school at the Douglass, played sports there as a teen, and volunteered at the Center while studying at Western Michigan University. The Rev. James Savory said there was no need to duplicate a community organizer position, and the church council proposed instead to work together and support Walker and the Douglass.

However, not soon after Walker began in June of 1967, Kal-Cap shared its funding outline during a community meeting. They planned to virtually suspend funding to the Douglass as they felt professionals, not "grassroots" organizers (as Walker had a master's degree), were on staff. Board members agreed to pay Walker with funds not provided by Kal-Cap in order to qualify for future grants earmarked for grassroots organizers to work in the community.

The mission of the Douglass as a place for the community was once applauded by funders. After the decreased attention to recreation and a subsequent increase in community problems, the Northside was being abandoned and those funds now were funneled to other neighborhoods. Walker's appointment was still fresh, and yet he had to prove he could make a difference for the sake of the organization.

Executive Director James Horn planned to run for the Board of Supervisors in the 1968 local elections. However, in October, he announced his withdrawal from the race and as director of the Douglass. The sudden move came with controversy that Horn was "being used as a tool of the White power structure to keep the Black community disorganized, divided and confused."

The allegations came amidst the resignations of Frank Ehlers and Nick Hall, director and deputy director respectively. The two were Kalamazoo Community Action Program officials. Of the allegations, Horn said:

"It's good for the people to realize—black and white, rich and poor—for any program to succeed, the people must be involved, must be aware of the goals that are set, the methods and techniques that are used to reach the goals, and must accept the programs that are developed through the involvement with people, and work cooperatively together."

Caldwell, now in his second term as the board president, accepted Horn's resignation. Other board members included: Creola Branscomb, vice president; Robert Travis, secretary; and Ruth Mitchell, treasurer.

The board felt there was no need to seek an outside candidate for the vacant director position. Walker was offered a promotion to lead the organization into the 50th anniversary and into the next decade. A 28-year-old Gil Bradley, an educator in the Kalamazoo Public Schools, came on as associate director.

As the two young men accepted their new positions, a huge financial "rug" was about to be pulled out from under their feet.

MAYOR GILBERT BRADLEY
A Plan For Action

BLACK HISTORY MONTH
HONORING LOCAL VOICES

GILBERT BRADLEY

- Elected Kalamazoo's first black and youngest mayor at 31 years of age, 1971.
- Director of Kalamazoo County Chamber of Commerce Human Development Department.
- Founding father of Alpha Phi Alpha Fraternity at WMU.
- Chairman of North Community Credit Union.
- Active with Big Brothers and Boy Scouts.
- Associate Director of Douglass Community Association.

Bourner's Gulf Service Station - 1221 N. Burdick Street, Kazoo

"It seems whenever we make a gain in one area, we receive a setback in another. Whatever shall we do—tell one-fifth of the people we are working with that we can't do anything for them any longer? If we can't get enough support to do the job right, I've got to question the whole existence of the agency."

Moses Walker

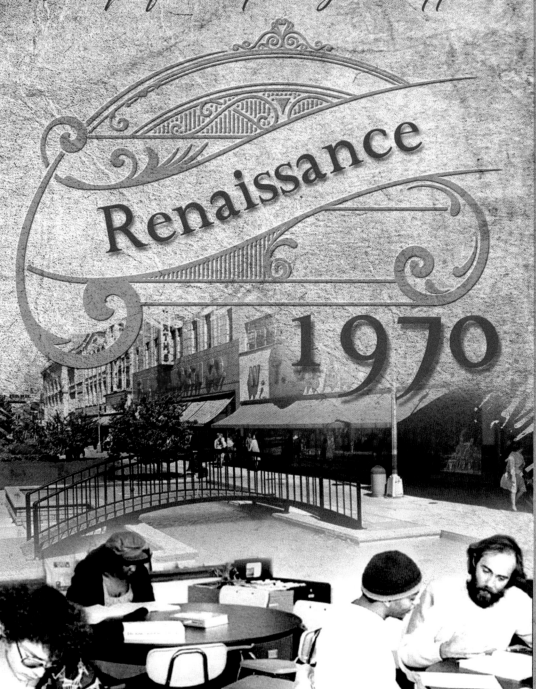

"When you fall asleep, things can happen."

Renaissance

1970

By 1970, after two years in the position, Moses Walker had settled in as director of the Douglass. The place where he had once attended nursery school was at a crossroads. Either he would succumb to the pressures of federal funders who held purse strings with compromising contingencies, or he would stand up for the people they served with courage. It was a tough decision he expressed in the media.

A constant stream of "philosophical" differences with the National Office of Economic Opportunity (OEO) led to them pulling their $26,000 funding (one-fifth of the organization's budget). The war on poverty funds by OEO came with endless red tape. While Walker and his staff worked with local governments to improve housing and job issues, the OEO wanted social workers in the field seeing as many individuals as possible. Walker said he wanted to provide a cure, not a band-aid, for families in the community.

Moses Walker had a connection to the Douglass from his youth. He brought new energy along with his staff pictured here in 1974. From left: Walker, Robert Straits, Gordon Brown, and Sonia Archer). (Kalamazoo Gazette/ Kalamazoo Central High School Online Yearbooks)

The goal was to fund the IntReFol program (INTake, REferral, and FOLlow-up) that would provide a social service model to the community. The agency made it clear that recreation would no longer be the focus of the Douglass in this collaboration. At the sacrifice of a safe place for more than 2,000 youth to take part in organized activities, the Center now serviced about 800 "cases" a month.

Walker and his twelve full-time and one part-time staff worked with individuals to help with issues of education, employment, and housing. The former snack bar where students had enjoyed sodas with their friends was now a Planned Parenthood clinic. The days of a center open from 9 a.m. to 11:30 p.m., a safe and welcoming place for students to take part in sports, clubs, and just be in the presence of educated role models, was just a collection of great memories.

In the meantime, the OEO's sudden withdrawal of funds in the fall of 1969 made way for others to step in to fill the gap. Those proponents of the Douglass, like the Kalamazoo Community Foundation and Community Chest, provided a financial safety net. The Foundation provided a $9,600 grant, and Community Chest upped its $45,500 grant in 1969 to a promise of $57,000 for 1970.

Money from these organizations allowed the work to move forward, work like that of the newly-created Job Development and Placement Program. While some areas of the community were reluctant to hire

Job Problems Discussed Here

KG 4-16-69

By ARTHUR SILLS, Gazette Staff Writer

Jobs were rated as a major concern at a Tuesday meeting on Kalamazoo's North Side.

The session was described as part of a program to seek "positive feedback" on problems within the Northside community.

Called by the Douglass Community Association (DCA), it also served as a citizens sounding board for the anti-poverty war being waged by the Kalamazoo County Community Action Program (Kal-Cap).

Board and staff members of both agencies formed a sizeable share of the 80 persons meeting at the DCA building.

Citizens were asked by Moses L. Walker, DCA director, if what it is "doing is meaningful and relevant to their lives."

Explaining, Walker said for 45 years after its 1919 founding, DCA was "oriented toward recreation" of blacks.

Since 1964, he said it "shifted its emphasis" to being "more beneficial, more meaningful" to the area it serves, primarily to "meet the needs of black people."

Its main work is carried in three programs, said Gilbert Bradley, DCA associate director:

● A service project that steers people with problems to agencies, then works to make sure they get aid.

● Job development and placement services that, last year put 207 of 361 job seekers to work.

● Housing help that includes a two-year-old project that has rehabilitated 38 homes.

The DCA building at 231 E. Ransom houses offices of the Planned Parenthood Association and the Northside Community Credit Union, along with state employment services.

About 45 per cent of the DCA operating funds come from the Community Chest, with the Civic Fund and the federal War on Poverty supplying most of the rest.

Most of the session's questions centered around employment, but recent rocktrowing incidents did stir one spectator.

He asked if an organization was checking into the rockthrowing by Northside teenagers.

"We're concerned about it as an organization," replied Walker, noting that it is problem that is going to need "the involvement of all the parents, all of the adults that live in the Northside area."

He said he saw hope in parental involvement in a unit named the Northside Committee for Educational Advancement, formed after disorders at Kalamazoo Central High School.

(In a post-meeting interview, Walker siad four recent committee meetings had drawn between 35 and 50 parents each.)

To one questioner, Bradley said most previous job placements have been on non-skilled jobs. There seems "some breaking through, but it's pretty rough," he added.

Applicants for craft union apprenticeships are "only a trickle," said Bradley. Many don't think they have a chance, he explained.

Blacks, Kalamazoo Contractors and Construction Trade Unions partnered for a training program. In addition, the Home Rehabilitation and Conservation programs founded in 1965 provided summer jobs and counseling.

In an annual report presented to the board on January 14, 1971, Walker outlined a plan to breathe new life into the organization. He would initiate meetings to secure more funding from a diverse pool of funders, increase support from Community Chest, and secure funds from the county for mental health services and human resources. He proposed a treatment center with funds from state and federal grants, and dreamed of a Northside medical facility.

Walker presented his "road map for the future," which would need the full support of the staff and board to come to fruition. For the next seven years he worked to maintain the aspects of this "map."

The organization's volunteers and board worked to preserve some of
the youth activities that were once the focus of the Center. The board
was led by Upjohn Co. microbiologist Dr. James P. Rolls, president;
Raymond Lett, vice president; Creola Branscomb, treasurer; and
Judy Lyons, secretary. In 1970 the third annual Head Start Christmas
party was held at the Douglass. Women volunteers from the community provided a Christmas party for nearly 100 Head Start students
with the help of fundraising and business contributions (*Kalamazoo
Gazette*, Dec. 13, 1970).

Job training and mental health became a focus
as some tried to maintain past traditions of the
Douglass' early years such as the annual Christmas parties for youth. (Douglass Community
Center Archives)

However, employment efforts reigned at the organization. The Michigan Employment Security Commission had a satellite site in the Center that offered manual labor jobs for $2 an hour and up (*Kalamazoo Gazette*, Oct. 19, 1971). Jobs were vital to the community, and at the same time racial hostilities brewed in a country still wounded by the 1968 assassinations of leaders such as the Rev. Dr. Martin Luther King, Jr., and Robert Kennedy, a presidential hopeful.

Kalamazoo was not exempt from racial tensions. In the past, the Douglass was a place for Blacks in the community to escape from prejudice. The social service focus of the organization needed to have a balance, and board president Dr. James P. Rolls felt the time had come. Shortly after his reelection as board president in 1971, he felt a Teen Center was needed and a "rededication to promoting the cause of Black people

Rev. Dr. Martin Luther King, Jr. during a press conference, 1964.(Library of Congress)

DOUGLASS
COMMUNITY
ASSOCIATION

(Douglass Community
Association Archives)

in our struggle to survive in a hostile society"
(*Kalamazoo Gazette*, June 25, 1971).

Walker heard Rolls and worked to find a balance. He was struggling to fund the agency's $151,605 budget with the support of grants from local foundations. The challenge to help people with basic needs and provide mental health service would take skill. His fund development took a new turn after a visit to a mental health clinic in Detroit, where he witnessed the basic needs of clients being met with the help of mental health counseling funds. The counseling efforts could now be more hands-on than ever before.

CONDUCTING RESEARCH FOR THE TENANTS HANDBOOK
Sandra Watson, David Johnson Find Vital Statistic

FINDING WHERE THE TROUBLE LIES
Michael Long, Mental Health Program Coordinator

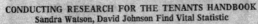

From The Bottom Up

That's How Douglass Community Association
Tackles Various Complexities Of Mental Health

In the *Kalamazoo Gazette* article "From the Bottom Up" (April 22, 1972), program coordinators summarize the new approach to the Center's efforts to support the entire family. The reporter is provided with the following scenario:

A woman comes into the center for help and shares that her husband's alcoholism is a detriment to the family finances and mental stability. Instead of just stopping at the counseling, they continue. Counselors provide budgeting tips and contact her creditors to arrange a payment plan. The husband is counseled by a member of the staff who is a recovering alcoholic for intervention.

Another counselor calls the husband's employer to explain the situation and that the husband is undergoing treatment, preventing his firing. As the husband is out of work, the family qualifies for food stamps, which a counselor helps the family secure. At the end, the wife has new respect for her husband, the financial pressures have eased, and the mental health of the family is improved.

By 1974 the Center was recognized for its comprehensive approach to mental health. Gordon Brown was hired as job development coordinator, and Sonia Archer of New York came on as community mental health coordinator. Both saw the new director of the Douglass as a "renaissance," according to a *Kalamazoo Gazette* article (Sept. 22, 1974).

Archer had a history of success in New York through her work with teenage gangs and as a prisoner advocate with the Attica Defense Committee. She had heard of Walker's efforts in Kalamazoo and wanted to be a part of his vision of a mentally healthy community. Brown realized many didn't approve of the Douglass changing its focus, but he believed helping the economically disadvantaged was more of a solution than the recreation focus of the past.

It was during the mid '70s that the face of those who entered the Center changed. Nearly 90 percent of the county residents were White, and federal funds for training attracted "more people who traditionally did not use Douglass Community Association," said Robert Straits, a manpower counselor at the time (*Kalamazoo Gazette*, Sept. 22, 1974).

In 1978, Walker was approached with the opportunity to take what he had learned as director of the Douglass and apply it on a city-wide scale as head of mental health at Borgess Methodist Hospital. He wasn't abandoning the community but positioning himself to do even more on a broader scale. Although the Douglass never established the medical facility he imagined, his new position with Borgess provided the knowledge, resources, and networking abilities that would benefit him as a board member of what would become the Family Health Center. In 1971 the medical clinic began in a mobile trailer in the city's Northside neighborhood.

In an interview in preparation for the 100th anniversary of the Douglass, Walker shared that, although he and many of his peers had grown up with a foundation rooted in the Douglass, the center had been more of a cultural center, not a social service agency. His role was to take it in a new direction, to help individuals and families through employment and mental health counseling.

When he stepped down from his role at the Douglass, the organization had an operating budget of $750,000. While he said he can't identify the basis for the financial struggles the organization had once he left, he has a theory. He felt those at the Douglass fell into complacency as the oldest Black-run organization in the community. He said leaders may have depended too much on those who provided over $100,000 in grants and funding and not enough on diverse funding streams and the cultivation of new partnerships and collaborations.

 "When you fall asleep, things can happen. When we don't provide direction to the young people and families in our community, we stop growing. Growth is the only sign of life."

Moses Walker passed away on January 16, 2020, not long after the author's interview with him for this book. His work in community health was recognized in 2017 when a 75,000-square-foot addition to the Family Health Center was renamed the Moses L. Walker Building.

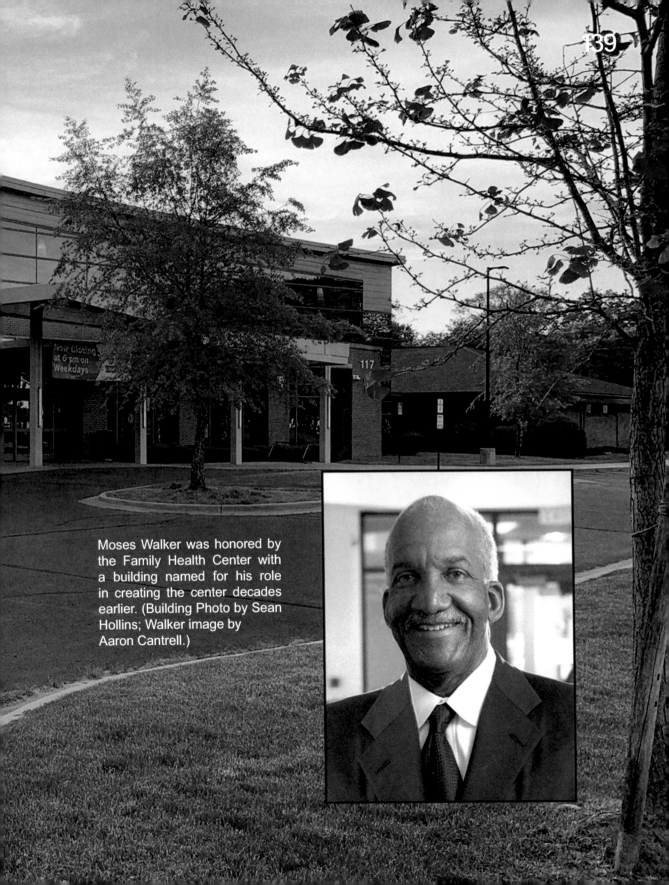

Moses Walker was honored by the Family Health Center with a building named for his role in creating the center decades earlier. (Building Photo by Sean Hollins; Walker image by Aaron Cantrell.)

"'Douglass Community Association...A New Beginning,' is appropriate and timely. We have an opportunity to make a new start, to use different approaches in solving old problems, to be creative and innovative in planning and implementing programs, and to seek greater community involvement and input."

Douglass Board of Directors, 1984

"When I was a child, Douglass was the agency for black people."

A New Beginning...Again

1980

DOUGLASS
COMMUNITY
ASSOCIATION

Jan Khabeiry was an administrative assistant for Moses Walker. A mother of twin boys in her thirties, Khabeiry left a position as secretary for Kalamazoo Public Schools to join the Douglass. Although she knew very little about the association, she was intrigued by the mission and felt she could bring her organizational skills to assist the director. She kept records in order as directors came and went. Gordon Brown joined as director in 1978, followed by Nathanial McCaslin in 1981. Before 1981 ended, Rick Frazier was named the new director.

Khabeiry and Frazier witnessed the financial challenges of running a social service agency while continuing to provide youth outreach. Donald Jackson, a coach with Kalamazoo Public Schools, was well-respected in the community for his stern yet well-meaning demeanor. His no-nonsense work ethic made him the ideal manager for the Home Rehabilitation and Conservation program, a program created in 1965 to provide skills to young workers and a beautification service to the community.

"I remember Douglass when the Home Rehabilitation and Conservation Program was a part of the old outreach summer program during the summer months of 1965. The program at that time was a "rag-tag" outfit with borrowed ladders that had to be carried to paint sites on the north side, but still the youth provided a worthwhile service to homeowners and gained valuable experience in the world of work," Jackson was quoted in the 1984 Douglass Souvenir Program.

The community takes part in the unveiling of a painting of Frederick Douglass by local artist Murphy Darden at the Douglass Community Association.(Douglass Community Center Archives)

Jackson, a Quincy, Illinois, native, came to Kalamazoo in 1960, during a time when the public schools began opening their doors to more minority educators. He began at Lincoln Junior High School on the city's Northside. The special education teacher brought his talents as a motivator and became a basketball coach. Hackett Catholic Central across town heard of his reputation as a coach and hired him to coach. In 1969 he led their team to the state finals.

Kalamazoo Public Schools wanted a basketball championship as well, so Jackson was rehired to coach at Kalamazoo Central High School. He became the first African American to coach at the district's high school level and led the school to ten conference championships and various state playoffs. His reputation as a coach and connection to local students made him a model leader for the Home Rehabilitation and Conservation program.

In the early days, the painters were young men assigned to homes on the city's East and North sides, mainly those of low-income senior citizens. Federal Housing and Urban Development (HUD) funds allowed the citizens to receive the service for free while the students were paid. Jackson was not only a mentor to the young men in the skill of painting, but also on how to respect seniors, how to carry themselves with pride, to work for an employer, and on how to work as a team. Men in the community such as teacher and coach Clarence Gardner also dedicated time to supervise the youth.

O'Neal Ollie was one of those young people who saw a job as a way to pay for his own school clothes or other needs. He was the youngest of eight children whose family lived a few blocks from the Ransom Street center. His roots ran deep with the Douglass, from Head Start

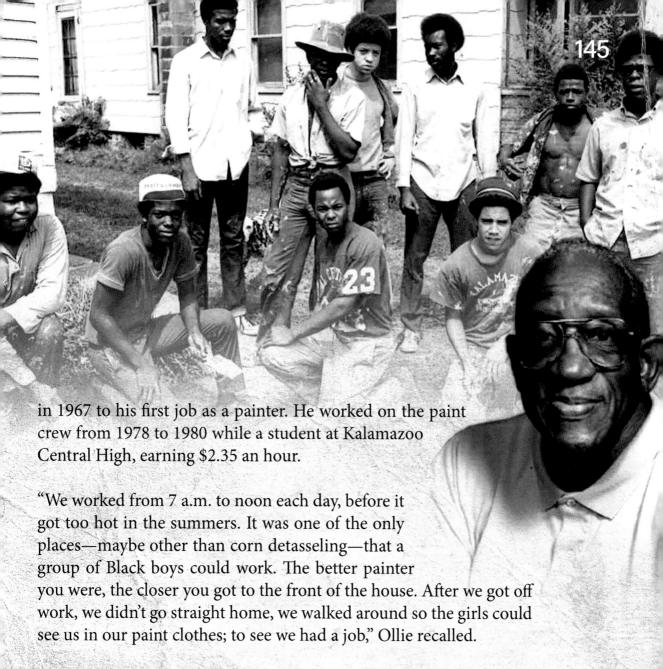

in 1967 to his first job as a painter. He worked on the paint crew from 1978 to 1980 while a student at Kalamazoo Central High, earning $2.35 an hour.

"We worked from 7 a.m. to noon each day, before it got too hot in the summers. It was one of the only places—maybe other than corn detasseling—that a group of Black boys could work. The better painter you were, the closer you got to the front of the house. After we got off work, we didn't go straight home, we walked around so the girls could see us in our paint clothes; to see we had a job," Ollie recalled.

After high school graduation, Ollie left for college in California, where he played basketball on scholarship and later earned a degree in business administration from California State University in San Bernardino. Just as he returned home in the summer of 1984, the new Center was completed at 1000 W. Paterson Street.

Donald Jackson served as a coach and supervisor to the young men of the Douglass Community Association. (Douglass Community Association Archives)

A New Home...Again

The $2.3 million dollar building was designed by Roger Margum to include space for a gymnasium, an all-purpose room, and a day care center. There was also a planned partnership with the Alma Powell Branch of the library to rent space at the new facility. The Alma Powell Branch had been located on North Burdick, in the former Van Avery Drugstore. Funds from foundations, businesses, and individuals made the new home one everyone could be proud of creating.

On October 27, 1984, hundreds of people from diverse backgrounds, ages, and economic status took part in an elaborate ceremony to unveil the new building. Musical selections and presentations from Boy Scout troops were on the ceremony agenda.

Hundreds came out to the grand opening of the new Douglass, 1984. (Douglass Community Association Archives) New Douglass image courtesy of Kalamazoo Public Library.

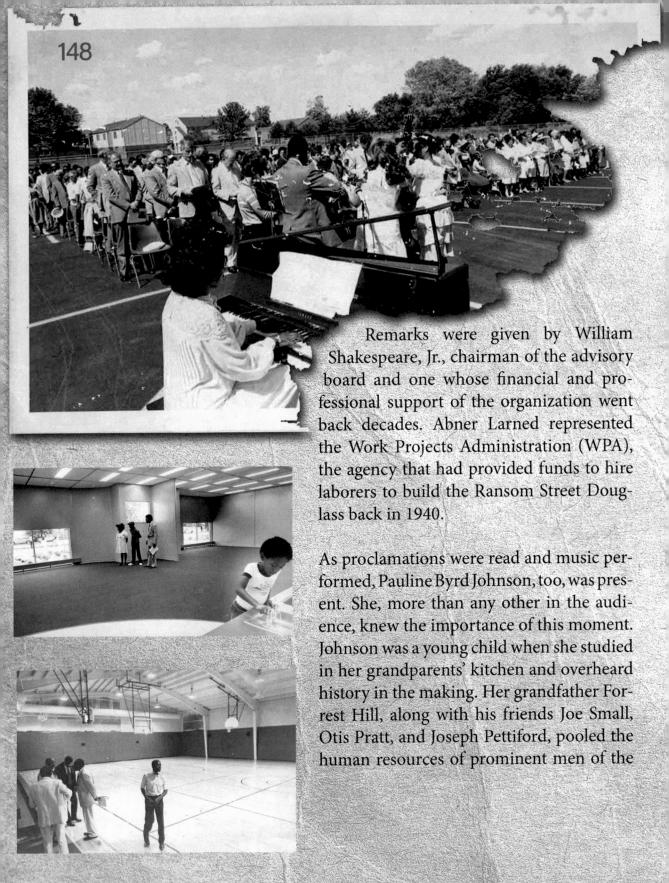

Remarks were given by William Shakespeare, Jr., chairman of the advisory board and one whose financial and professional support of the organization went back decades. Abner Larned represented the Work Projects Administration (WPA), the agency that had provided funds to hire laborers to build the Ransom Street Douglass back in 1940.

As proclamations were read and music performed, Pauline Byrd Johnson, too, was present. She, more than any other in the audience, knew the importance of this moment. Johnson was a young child when she studied in her grandparents' kitchen and overheard history in the making. Her grandfather Forrest Hill, along with his friends Joe Small, Otis Pratt, and Joseph Pettiford, pooled the human resources of prominent men of the

community to form the Douglass Community Association in 1919. Wealthy White men with names such as Gilmore, Upjohn, and Edward Desenburg (Pretty Lake Camp founder) were recruited for financial support. What began as a place for Colored soldiers from Camp Custer in Battle Creek had become a community safe haven for all ages.

The men at that table may not have imagined the magnitude of their dream, not only for the Douglass, but for their children and grandchildren. Hill's granddaughter, Pauline, made history in 1926 as the first African American female graduate of Kalamazoo College and the first African American elementary teacher hired by Kalamazoo Public Schools. She volunteered her time to the Douglass in every building it was ever housed. She diligently served as a volunteer for everything from story time with toddlers to being the first female to head the organization's board of directors.

Small's son Clarence became an accomplished musician and music teacher. He was known near and far for his skills on the violin, drums, and piano. Otis Pratt's youngest son graduated from Kalamazoo Central High School in 1928 and soon left in his Ford Model T to Howard University in Washington, D.C. He earned both a Bachelor of Arts in Teaching (1932) and a degree in law from Howard in 1935. Pratt returned to Kalamazoo and opened a law practice on the same floor as the Douglass Community Center, then located on South Burdick, above Lakey's Paint Store. After a brief stint as a captain in the Army, he returned home, continued his practice, and in 1968 became the county's first African American judge.

The dedication of the new building may have meant more to Johnson than to the little kids who would run in its massive gym or to the adults who would receive social services. In the meantime, mental health continued to be a priority for the organization, with the Rev. Guyron Philbert leading that aspect of programming. By the mid 1980s, summer job programs were not just an option, they were vital to the well-being of some African American boys in cities across the country.

See page 6 for a guide to local events

KALAMAZOO NEWS

THE INDEPENDENT WEEKLY 15¢

Volume Five, Number 28   Mail Subscriptions Available for $10.00 Per Year   Phone 342-1973   Feb. 24–March 1, 1984

Public Trust Trampled

City Chided For Giving Road To P...

Pauline Johnson in 1922

Lone Wolf Still Active

Editor's note: Many people today know Pauline Byrd Johnson from her lively input at City Commission meetings. Her integrity, tenacious spirit, humor, and outspokenness have delighted many City Hall audiences. She represents some of Kalamazoo's best history, and it seems appropriate to share part of it as we celebrate Black History Month. Most of the following article is based on excerpts from "Lone Wolf" by Ruth Ann Moerdyk, published in Emancipated Spirits: Portraits of Kalamazoo College Women (1983, Gail Griffin, Josephine Casto, Ruth Moerdyk, and Cheryl Lieser).

A turning point in Pauline Johnson's life came in the 10th grade at Central High shortly after World War One. It was then that her government teacher, Nellie Roewarena, introduced her to the Declaration of Independence. She was "walking on air for a long time" after discovering the passage that said, "We hold these truths to be self-evident, that all men are created equal." She had never heard that before from a white person. Young Pauline made up her mind then that since she was equal, she would act the part no matter where, no matter what.

Continued on page 5

February 24, 1984   KALAMAZOO NEWS THE INDEPENDENT WEEKLY   Page 5

Pauline Johnson was a pioneer in local integration movement

Continued from page 1

Mrs. Johnson's great grandfather, Robert Bradley, was the son of his owner. His mother was a woman whom George Bradley, a wealthy plantation owner in Kentucky, apparently loved. They had six or seven children. George Bradley was good to his mistress and kept these children on his plantation to keep them safe and to educate them. When Robert Bradley was a young man he fell in love with a slave girl on another plantation and his father bought her so they could marry. As Civil War clouds gathered, George Bradley convinced his bi-racial children, who were all grown by then, that they must go north. He gave each of them gold, money, free papers, and outfitted them with covered wagons and whatever they needed. Mrs. Johnson says his goodbye message included this: "It doesn't matter what anybody says or does; remember, you are the aristocrats."

Robert Bradley and his family bought a farm in Oshtemo on what is now Parkview Ave. One of his children, Flora, married Forrest Hill in 1872. Flora and Forrest were Pauline's grandparents. She says, "They had a lovely married life. She was just as gentle and placid as my grandfather was aggressive. But as ladylike as she was, when it came down to it, she had an awful lot of power and influence over that big he-man, and he respected her very much, very much." Grandpa Hill was from a family in Niles that had never been enslaved. He was a hard-working, intelligent man who managed his financial affairs in such a way that he always could save part of his earnings, and was well liked when he retired from years of self-employment as a contractor in Kalamazoo. This man is Pauline Johnson's hero.

One of Flora and Forrest's children was Edith Belle Hill, Pauline's mother. After she married and had two children by Oscar Byrd, he announced that he was still in love with his childhood sweetheart, and left Edith to raise the children. Pauline glows with love and admiration while speaking of her mother, as does Mrs. Johnson's daughter, Joanne Allison, when she recalls her grandmother. Edith and her two children went to live with Flora and Forrest until Edith could get on her feet financially. Being a single parent at the turn of the century was not in vogue. Edith's struggle and strength deeply inspired her daughter.

Though she had no contact with her father besides a brief visit to his home years later, the Byrd family is a source of pride for Mrs. Johnson. Abner Byrd, her grandfather, fought in the Civil War—"I was very proud of that because it took initiative and effort and patriotism, things that I think are appropriate." She recalls that the Byrd family had a reputation of fighting the slave catchers who came to the Cass County area. A large portion of the early white settlers there were Quakers who soon linked themselves with the Underground Railroad; as a result many free Negroes and runaway slaves settled in this area.

"The fact that they had character and the courage either to run away, or if they were free, to leave slave territory, where they would be safer," Mrs. Johnson says, "shows a good deal of independence and determination to be what America stood for. I think they had that although they weren't educated; in the air were equality and justice and fair play for everybody, and they intended to have it."

Pauline Byrd was born Feb. 5, 1904 in Bronson Hospital. Soon after she moved into her grandparents' home, a pattern of being alone began to develop. At age 4 or 5, the death of her brother and playmate, Ogden, contributed to her solitariness. Her grandparents had a farm on what is now Pioneer St., in an all white area. Even though her family gave her much love and attention, the absence of childhood companions was a real loss to her.

Grandma Bradley and Pauline had daily discussions in which education was portrayed as the biggest ideal to live for. Pauline attended Vine Street School through the eighth grade, and graduated from Central High in 1922. During most of those years, she was the only black in class. Although she was bright and active, the children did not include her, so she turned to reading to pull herself through the social isolation.

Pauline's mother gave her a sense of thrift and economy. Edith had become a hairdresser who went to wealthy women's homes. She saved enough money to buy a house on Millview Ave. in the Westnedge Hill area when Pauline started high school. "Once a week, Saturday night," Pauline remembers, "we would sit at the kitchen table and my mother would empty out the money she had made that week. She would then make little piles: one for taxes,

one for fuel, one for food, one for clothing, one for church, and then, the last one—if there was any left—was for my education. If after all that there was any left over, we could walk downtown and see a movie, a rare treat."

In addition to occupying herself with studies and babysitting, Pauline also took piano and voice lessons for most of her youth. She spent a lot of time in activities around the Douglass Community Center (her grandfather was one of the founders) during her high school years. She wasn't accepted by her high school peers, and the young people at the Center didn't fully accept her, either.

It was about this time in her life when a bitter injustice was thrust on her. She can't recall the details, but she was so upset she developed a backache that kept her bedridden for three days. It dawned on her that the person who mistreated her hadn't been hurt a bit, and here she was with a terrible backache because she got so angry. She asked herself, "Now are you going to let other people make you suffer like that for the mean things they do?" And the answer, "No, this is the end. I'll never let anyone affect me this way again. I understand what is making you horrid, and I am not going to let that control me. I'm not going to let injustice or greed or selfishness or prejudice affect me. When you have control of yourself you have control of the world; the world can't bother you."

Mrs. Johnson entered Kalamazoo College in 1922. She wanted to go south to a "colored" university where she could not only get an education but also have some fun. Her family was very committed to integration, however, and insisted that Pauline "learn to think and act and talk and do everything with white people. If

Pauline Johnson today

you go south to a colored school you're going to be separating yourself from the general population." So, against her desires, she became the first black ever at K-College.

Again Pauline was excluded from social events. And the gap between her and her own race continued to grow, as it was considered silly and stupid to go on to school. She became a lone wolf, burying herself in studies every night. Her mother's conversion to Christian Science further isolated her from community Negroes.

After graduating from K-College in 1926 as a certified teacher, she went to the University of Chicago for one year to study social work, but soon realized she didn't like that profession. Following a brief job with a "colored" YWCA in Ohio, Pauline came home and attended Western for one semester before accepting her first teaching job—in Cass County. It was 1929, and she found herself teaching in the very school her father had attended, a one-room, eighth-grade school. She learned quickly to put most of her energy into organizing the 7th and 8th graders and encouraged the younger ones to study with each other, the 5th graders reading to the third graders, and so on.

During that year she heard of a school near Louisville, Kentucky (Lincoln Ridge Junior College), a school for college-age black youths. Whitney Young, Sr. was the principal and Pauline became a teacher to his son, whom she considered to be a brilliant child. She kept up correspondence with Whitney Young, Jr. over the years.

She only stayed at Lincoln Ridge for a year. Being barred from the local public library on the basis of color was more than she cared to accept. She objected to the social set-up of Louisville, and realized she could be in danger with her radical ideas, such as looking white people in the eye, a practice that was not tolerated by whites then and there.

Pauline returned to Kalamazoo, did volunteer work at Douglass Center, and there she met Chester Taylor. They married, and in 1933 Pauline became a mother to Edith Joanne Taylor. Marriage and motherhood did not fit well on Pauline, however—"I did something I've always been ashamed of: I divorced him." She could not deny her strong drive to continue to her career, and although her husband had done nothing wrong, she just couldn't face a life of sweeping and getting meals and childcare. Pauline's mother loved Joanne, so she became the baby's main provider, freeing Pauline up to continue her career.

Pauline applied to and was accepted at a Negro high school in Gary, Indiana, a big school with an all-Negro staff. She worked with teenagers from deprived backgrounds, and learned how to break through their indifference and get them involved with the business of learning. She told stories to get the students to quiet down and listen for a

Continued on page 12

The Kalamazoo News featured Pauline Johnson, whose grandfather, Forrest Hill, helped found Frederick Douglass Center in 1919. (Digital Michigan Newspapers - Central Michigan University)

Keeping Youth Safe

The new Douglass couldn't have come to the Northside community at a better time. Cocaine was being repurposed into crack, a more affordable, easy-to-create, highly-addictive substance. Street wars over drug turf grew intensely violent across the country, particularly in neighborhoods where drug lords had set up shop. Laws that targeted both sellers and users of crack led to an increase in incarceration. Some young men saw drug dealing as a way to earn fast money to buy the material things they otherwise could not obtain through a minimum wage salary (if they could even get a job).

In an attempt to find a solution, in 1985 President Ronald Reagan signed the Anti-Drug Abuse Act, designating federal funds for inner city programs to curb drug-related crime and usage. Programs such as Drug Abuse Resistance Education (DARE) strove to teach kids to "Just Say No" to drugs.

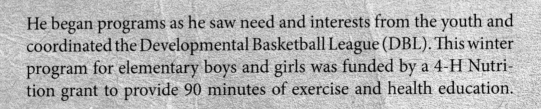

O'Neal Ollie returned to the community and was hired in 1986 by director Rick Frazier as a full-time recreation coordinator. Initially, he was in charge of opening the gym for kids to have a place to play. He also managed the paint program he had benefited from as a teen.

He began programs as he saw need and interests from the youth and coordinated the Developmental Basketball League (DBL). This winter program for elementary boys and girls was funded by a 4-H Nutrition grant to provide 90 minutes of exercise and health education.

The YBL came next (**Y.M.C.A.**, **Boys** Scouts of America, **L**incoln Elementary School), targeting middle-school aged boys. That program was taken over by the Hoopsters, a group of African American men in the community who managed the teams. What began as a project of Mike Williams, Andre Baraka, and Van Ollie merged into one led by those such as Gus Calbert, Alex Walker, Arthur Truss, Don Jackson, Clarence Gardner, and Dick Brown and was later adopted by the Douglass.

Calbert, along with other board members and men in the community, were faithful volunteers at the Douglass. O'Neal Ollie counted on the men (after a long day on their own jobs) to meet with young boys after school for tutoring and sports. Terri Benton-Ollie (O'Neal's wife) secured women from her local Alpha Kappa Alpha Sorority to help tutor. Lori Bell worked with the young cheerleaders on self esteem and cheer routines for Rocket football games.

Rocket football became the most successful program the Douglass organized, with thousands of girls and boys participating as football players or cheerleaders for nearly twenty-five years. The program was at its peak in 1988 with three teams per age group for players and up to fifty cheerleaders from third grade and higher. Each weekday, the participants met at the Douglass for tutoring and presentations by local mentors before practice began. On Saturdays, the students put their skills to the test through competitions with local and nearby teams.

Left: O'Neal Ollie huddles with players before a game. Above: Men in the community volunteer to mentor and coach students who participate in basketball and football programs at the Douglass. (Douglass Community Center Archives)

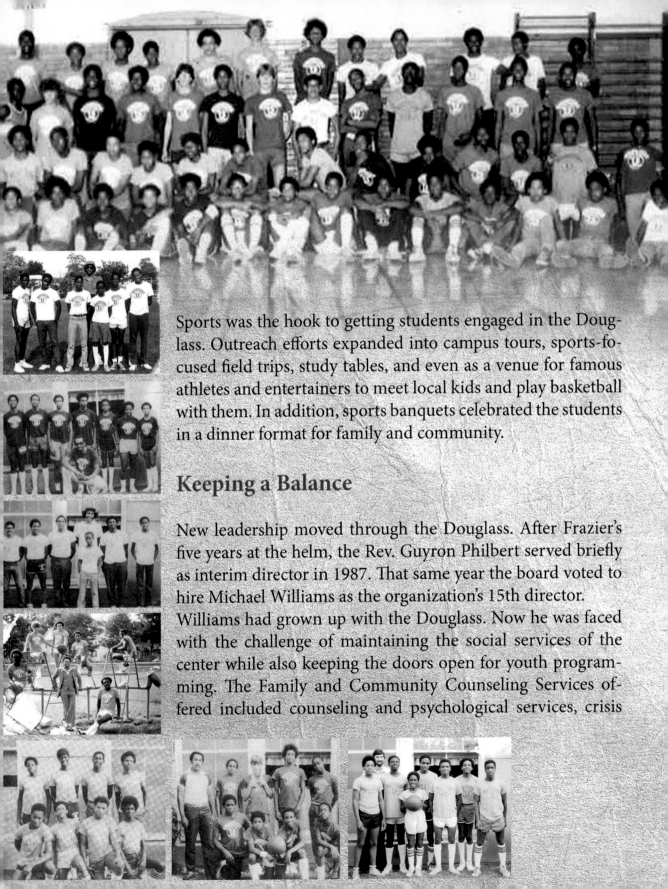

Sports was the hook to getting students engaged in the Douglass. Outreach efforts expanded into campus tours, sports-focused field trips, study tables, and even as a venue for famous athletes and entertainers to meet local kids and play basketball with them. In addition, sports banquets celebrated the students in a dinner format for family and community.

Keeping a Balance

New leadership moved through the Douglass. After Frazier's five years at the helm, the Rev. Guyron Philbert served briefly as interim director in 1987. That same year the board voted to hire Michael Williams as the organization's 15th director. Williams had grown up with the Douglass. Now he was faced with the challenge of maintaining the social services of the center while also keeping the doors open for youth programming. The Family and Community Counseling Services offered included counseling and psychological services, crisis counseling, psychiatric services, STEP (Stepping Toward Employment Potential) for adults, along with tutoring for those in grades 6-12, a Free Store of clothing and other home items, along with the nearly 30 year-old home rehabilitation summer job program.

The role of the director had expanded over the years as well as the perception of who the Douglass served.

"When I was a child, Douglass was the agency for black people," Williams said in a 1998 *Kalamazoo Gazette* article, "Center Has Played a Pivotal Role." "There was a time when it needed to be all to everybody. That to a degree has changed."

As the 1980s came to a close, the Douglass had begun a shift back toward more recreation than social services. Youth and the dozens of dedicated volunteers became the face of the Douglass. What began in 1919 for African American soldiers of Camp Custer had evolved over the years as a recreational facility that was recognized for curbing crime among young people. The social service and employment focuses benefited the community; however, youth intervention was the lifeline of the new Douglass.

DOUGLASS
COMMUNITY
ASSOCIATION

"It was around the late '40s, early '50s when I quit school in the ninth grade to work to help my family. I shined shoes at the Hilton for tips.

We weren't welcome at the YMCA, but the Douglass was where I could go to meet my friends. There was a room where young men could hang out, and one for young ladies. Then we would all go down to the basement to play pool, ping pong, and cards. There was a snack bar down there, too. Gospel entertainers would do concerts and on Fridays there were dances.

My fondest memories were playing basketball there and having my girlfriend Vera (now wife) watch me."

Renaford Owens, Sr.

"Whole purpose of Midnight League was to prevent things like this."

Douglass - A Safe Haven

1990

From North Burdick to Ransom to Paterson streets, the Douglass was a place where people of color were not treated as second-class citizens. It was a place to dance, laugh, play, and learn. The staff and volunteers had a mission to help them succeed in whatever job or career they dreamed. It was a place where college-educated mentors stood up for, and with, them.

Juanita Goodwin was one of those mentors. In 1943 she arrived from Arizona after completing high school. She eventually graduated from Western Michigan University and worked as the Girls' director of the Douglass on Ransom Street. She later became a teacher in Kalamazoo Public Schools and made history as the first African American female principal in the city. Her work at the Douglass provided youth with new opportunities to expand their horizons through sports and clubs while providing them with leadership skills and a sense of pride.

"I wanted to prepare them so when the door (of opportunity) opened they could slide through," she said in 1998 during an interview with the *Kalamazoo Gazette*.

By the 1990s, the organization seemed to be coming full circle as a hub for community activity for all ages. A multi-purpose room allowed for everything from weddings to summer lunch programs. The Kalamazoo Public Library housed the Alma Powell

The Kalamazoo Public Library's Alma Powell Branch has served as a partner to provide educational support to students who attend the Center for recreation.
(Douglass Community Center Archives)

branch in the Center. And a full-size gym allowed for basket-ball games for youth and area police, giving the police and young people the chance to meet and compete on the court.

Michael Williams had served as the executive director since 1987. He shared in his annual report that, by 1991, more than 2,400 had been benefited from the Douglass' Family and Community Counseling, Sickle Cell Counseling, Home Rehabilitation for Seniors, and Youth and Adult Recreation services, which included a Midnight Basketball League program for males ages 18-25.

Williams, like other executive directors before him, accredited the leadership of the board of directors for guiding the direction of the Douglass. That year George Dunn was board president, Malcolm Earhart was vice president, followed by Bill Goodman and Albert Little as treasurer and secretary, respectively. Others on the board included Ressie Brown, Jackie Cantrell, Walter Hall, William Roland, Gersteen Sherrod, Arthur Washington, Nancy Woods, Walt Worthy, and Gus Calbert.

The Douglass was a safe haven. Other community centers across the country had that reputation, as well. So when crimes related to drugs increased, the Anti-Crime Bill was signed in 1994 by President Bill Clinton to allocate millions of dollars to support programs in community recreation centers, such as the Midnight Basketball League.

Statistics showed that most crime in the inner-cities happened between the hours of 10 p.m. and 2 a.m. Local law enforcement

provided the numbers for Kalamazoo: Eighty percent of those arrested for crimes committed during those hours were African American males between the ages of 18 and 22. Because community centers had the support and connection to the community, millions were poured into them through the Anti-Crime Bill for programs like the Midnight Basketball League.

Leagues were formed as a way to get young people off the street, expose them to mentors, and provide college scholarships. The men could only play in a game if they were present at least thirty minutes beforehand for the pre-game presentation by a male in the community who had inspiration and wisdom to share.

Orlando Little was one of the stars of the Midnight League. A native of Kalamazoo, he came from a middle class family who valued education and a good work ethic. He had begun playing basketball at the Douglass' YBL program where his uncle Nate White was a volunteer coach. Little went on to graduate high school and received a scholarship from the Midnight League funds. While attending Kalamazoo Valley Community College toward a career as a detective, he worked as a security guard at Borgess Hospital.

On the night of a league championship for which his team had qualified to play, he decided to forgo the game and head to a local club, the Bachelor 14. A road rage confrontation led to him nearly killing another young man. At 18 years old, he was arrested and faced nearly thirty years in prison if the man died. The man survived and Little took a plea deal and served less than three years in prison for attempted manslaughter.

Top Left: Michael Williams (Douglass Community Center Archives)

Orlando Little grew up playing sports at the Douglass

"Whole purpose of Midnight League was to prevent things like this," Little said. "When I got out of prison I had a felony. I couldn't get a job and my family was disappointed in me. But, Ollie and others at the Douglass embraced me. I took part in MBL my last eligible year (age 22) and they used me as a poster-child to share my story with other players on what not to do and the consequences."

Little said his felony prevented him from getting a job anywhere, but the Douglass provided him with a chance to volunteer with the Rocket football program; that opportunity changed his life. He went on to work with other coaches to provide leadership to young boys through sports. He helped with homework, advocated for students with their teachers, and organized a sports banquet for the youth at the Radisson Plaza Hotel. The support from those at the Douglass led to him volunteering on various community organization boards and using his life experiences to help youth at Lakeside Academy for Youth in Kalamazoo.

"If it wasn't for the Douglass I don't know how my situation after prison would have ended. The more I talk about it, Douglass was the saving grace that helped me be successful today," Little said.

Ollie said it was a norm that the doors were open to youth with programs from 9 a.m. to 2 a.m. From youth programs in the mornings to high school basketball programs in the evening, the Douglass was a revolving door of activity that students took ownership in. Board members were in full support of the organization and its role in the community. Board

Some Douglass athletes went on to play college and professional sports. Counter clockwise: Duane Young, T.J. Duckett, Chris Crawford and Greg Jennings. Images courtesy of the Douglass Community Association.

members in 1991 included: George Dunn, president; Malcolm Earhart, vice president; Bill Goodman, treasurer; Albert Little, secretary; Ressie Brown, Gus Calbert, Jackie Cantrell, Walter Hall, William Roland, Gersteen Sherrod, Arthur Washington, Nancy Woods, and Walt Worthy. Many of the board members also served as volunteers for the youth programs.

Time would prove the impact the programs had on the students. The Northside Rocket football program included players such as Todd Jeffrey "TJ" Duckett who played for the Atlanta Falcons and Washington Redskins. Greg Jennings went on to play for the Greenbay Packers, Minnesota Vikings, and Miami Dolphins. Duane Young played for the San Diego Chargers and Buffalo Bills. Other students went on to play for college programs, like Camerron Cheatham who played for the University of Cincinnati.

Football wasn't the only program that inspired personal triumphs. The Midnight Basketball

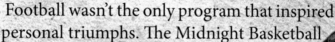

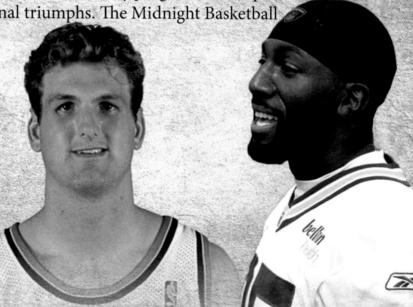

League also produced such success stories as those of Chris Crawford, who went on to play for Marquette University and later for the Atlanta Hawks. Fenorris Pearson earned a master's degree in Organizational Development and Management. As he reflected on his accomplishments, he realized the mentors and philanthropists he met through the Douglass Community Association played a key role in his success.

Gus Calbert, however, left a lifelong impact on Pearson, who grew up a few blocks from the center. He was among the first youth to hit the brand new basketball court as a member of YBL and later the Midnight Basketball League. Calbert was like a second father to Pearson. When he needed a ride to his job at McDonald's, Calbert loaned him his car. When he had a date, Calbert let him use the car to take her to the movies or dinner. Fittingly, it was Calbert's advice that stuck with him the most.

"He was always in my ear," Pearson said. "He would ask me, 'What will you do if you get hurt playing basketball? Get that education.' Those words were always in the back of my head."

Pearson heeded the advice. At the same time, one of his teammates, Jeff Olson, also played on the Amateur Athletic Union (AAU) basketball team at the Douglass. The two boys from different sides of the economic track became friends. Jeff's family invited Pearson to stay the night at their home, the first time he had ever stayed with a White family. Jeff's father, Wally, sponsored the team of teenagers on a trip to Stockholm, Sweden, to see a Volvo Cup professional basketball playoff. From the excitement of obtaining a passport to the experience of new foods, Pearson was forever changed.

"That trip led me to dream about traveling the world," Pearson said. "I ended up doing just that."

Through a scholarship program for men of the Midnight Basketball League, Pearson earned a full-ride basketball scholarship to Eastern Michigan University. He graduated from EMU in 1993 with a Bachelor of Science in Organizational Communication and Management. He later earned a Master of Science in Organizational Development and Management from Benedictine University. His work as a senior executive for two Fortune 500 companies (Motorola and Dell) and as a best-selling author has taken him across the globe.

Pearson remembers what the men of the Douglass did for him and has vowed to pay it forward. Through his position at Dell, he has pledged to provide computers to the Douglass, as well as internships and scholarships.

Success stories like those of Pearson are what led some local women to action. While the "new" Douglass worked to serve social service needs, they wanted to bring a focus back on the aspects they treasured

Center has played a pivotal

role

In its early years, Douglass Community Center was one of the few gathering places for black residents outside of church.

BY CEDRIC RICKS
KALAMAZOO GAZETTE

Vivian King and Arthur Dungy grew up during an era when blacks in Kalamazoo were limited to the least desirable jobs, faced restrictions in housing and weren't exactly welcomed in many restaurants and stores.

But one place where they always felt at home was the Douglass Community Center.

The center sponsored basketball teams during the years when blacks weren't welcome at the YMCA. It had a malt shop where the soda jerks didn't use a separate set of glasses for blacks. It had dances, theater performances and various clubs and events that embraced African-American culture.

In later years, when times changed, the Douglass center changed, too, shifting its focus from recreation to offering social services as Kalamazoo's black population suddenly grew in the post-war boom.

The history of the Douglass center is, in effect, the history of Kalamazoo's black community for the past eight decades.

"Douglass was as much a part of our lives as school was a part of our lives," said Moses Walker, a former Kalamazoo city commissioner and a past executive director of Douglass. "It was a pillar for the black community in the '40s, '50s and '60s."

Today, Douglass remains unique in the Kalamazoo community —

Michael Williams

more than a social agency, more than a recreational center and more than a neighborhood association.

"In many ways we are still perceived as a black agency," said Michael Williams, the center's executive director. "In many ways we are, but we are also serving the larger community."

Yet racial politics have always had an impact on Douglass – and, in fact, were responsible for its formation.

Opened in 1919, the Douglass Community Center was created for black soldiers stationed at what was then called Camp Custer, which was located between Kalamazoo and Battle Creek. The idea was to give soldiers, who were barred from many establishments because of their color, a place to socialize.

Blacks initiated the idea but raised the money from some of Kalamazoo's most prominent whites. When the center opened in the upstairs of a building on North Burdick Street, the association had a black board of directors – overseen by a white advisory board.

Douglass, which bears the name of the black abolitionist Frederick Douglass, quickly became a

gathering spot for Kalamazoo's small black community, which numbered fewer than 800 in 1920.

Vivian King, 79, and her brother, Arthur Dungy, 81, remember the center's early days.

"They had lots of activities going on at the Douglass Community Center, especially on the weekends," said King. "We would have basketball games. We had a juke box and a jam session

afterward."

Douglass offered study, sewing, and craft clubs for black women. Local residents also enjoyed Douglass' dances, sock dances, musical performances by the Douglass Dance Guild.

Douglass also sponsored basketball and various clubs for young black men.

"Blacks were not allowed in the YMCA," said Dungy. That began to change in his high school days, he said. "But before that, if you went into the 'Y' the guy who worked the desk would come over and tell you that you can't come in. But for Douglass the center offered more than just organized activities.

"Even if there wasn't anything special going on," he said, "it was just the camaraderie that I enjoyed."

In 1941, the center moved to a new facility built with assistance from the Works Progress Administration at the corner of Paterson and Pitcher streets. The center was a showplace. But it also was a reminder of segregation.

A fast city study on Kalamazoo's black population noted the ambiguous role some felt toward Douglass.

"It was a step forward and a step backward," a study quoted an unnamed black resident as saying. "The center has brought our people together, given us some consciousness. If it did the police them night. And for the are here to go the police."

Vivian King

Arthur Dungy

Children sit at tables in the Douglass Community Center nursery in the early '40s.
PHOTO COURTESY OF KALAMAZOO VALLEY MUSEUM

Yet the Douglass staff was determined to shield young blacks from the harsh realities of the times and to prepare them for something better.

"We tried to teach them and expose them to other things," said Juanita Goodwin, who said Juanita Goodwin, a longtime coordinator with Jobs for the center. "We then taught them how to dance. That was when people would come and be sold with a chuckle.

Goodwin said she wanted Douglass to exceed the lowest goals. One war for students to high school.

"I wanted to prepare them so when the door of opportunity opened they could slide through," said Goodwin.

Goodwin also showed the keen interest in social service, a critical need for blacks, as well as local staffing the had the offer rights for blacks to share a wrong night. The craft staff and all what for the are here to and Goodwin hate you did.

now that the Douglass City Center was a very

Douglass shifts focus

By 1960, Kalamazoo's black population had grown across from within two decades to over 5,500 residents – primarily the result of black migration from the South.

A growing civil rights movement was gathering steam nationally and having an impact in Kalamazoo.

As the trends had significant and opposite effects on Douglass.

As segregation began to crumble and restaurants, hotels, clubs and other public institutions took welcome black residents, Douglass' role as a social center lessened.

The old Paterson center on designed for the office space that now are needed, in group had to be sacrificed for the administrative space.

"When it was built as a WPA project it was as a recreational center," said Michael Williams, the center's current executive director. "When I was a child Douglass was the agency for people.

"There was a time when it needed to be all to everybody. That is changing.

because the stuff being discussed is confidential."

But moving from recreational to social services agency didn't come without resistance. It angered some of the older Douglass fans who felt the agency wasn't being true to its original mission.

"It just came down, a space become and prioritizing and have a job, they may not be able to be seen as a black agency," said Juanita Goodwin.

Goodwin, "The people who worked there know almost all the kids in the city."

Douglass shifts focus

Juanita Goodwin

Please see **DOUGLASS, C3**

of the "old" Douglass on Ransom Street. In 1998, the Merry Makers embarked on a renovation effort to revise the center with a recreation focus.

Gladys Fannin led the charge. She, along with her friends Alma Rancifer, Martha Brooks, Mary McCants, Rosa Lee White, and Needa Lockett, unlocked the center that had been abandoned 15 years earlier. They were shocked to see the building, once an architectural standout, now in desperate need of revitalization. Mount Zion Baptist Church had acquired the building and agreed to sell it to the women under a land contract. The Merry Makers invested $104,000 into a roof that was in complete disrepair. The gym that was once a hub for lavish banquets and musicals looked as if a bulldozer had destroyed it. The cleanup effort alone, before any renovations could be made, was $15,000.

DOUGLASS COMMUNITY CENTER

■ **1919:** Douglass Community Center opens on the second floor of a building on North Burdick Street to serve black soldiers stationed at nearby Camp Custer.

■ **1920-1940:** Center is a social hub for Kalamazoo's small black community.

■ **1941:** With help from the federal Works Progress Administration, new Douglass Community Center is constructed at the corner of Ransom and Pitcher streets.

■ **1942-1983:** The new Douglass Community Center expands beyond recreational activities to offer services such as job training and housing assistance as the area's black population swells due to Southern migration.

■ **1984:** A new Douglass Community Center is constructed at 1000 W. Paterson. The larger facility allows for more social programs, such as mentorship programs for young people and counseling, health services and programs for elderly and low-income residents.

■ **1998:** The Merry Makers begin renovating the old Douglass Community Center at Ransom and Pitcher streets for use as a community resource center.

They were looking at a price tag of more than $400,000 (*Kalamazoo Gazette*, Sept. 12, 1999).

WAYNE ANDERSON / GAZETTE

Today the gym is in need of major repairs but the Merry Makers, a local women's organization, is slowly making progress in its efforts to renovate the building. Two of the group's members, pictured in the photo above, inspect the new roof placed on the structure at Pitcher and Ransom streets.

In the article, Rancifer realized their dream was a big undertaking, but she said, "It would be a shame to do away with a part of Kalamazoo's history when this building could be renovated."

Funds for the Douglass were tight and any efforts to revamp the former building were not a priority. So the Merry Makers soldiered on to raise funds one bake sale, one bingo game, and one dinner at a time. After a valiant effort, they were unable to see their dream come to fruition.

Resurrecting the old Douglass center

WAYNE ANDERSON / GAZETTE

Gladys Fannin, president of the Merry Makers, leads members of her group on a tour of the old Douglass Community Center. Joining her are Kalamazoo residents Needa Lockett, center, and Rosa Lee

"Today, our kids begin to use computer devices and phones as early as their young hands can hold them. So we must keep up with the times by providing students access to the same type of technology they use in school to do their homework. As society's needs change, we plan to continue to adjust to accommodate those requirements."

Sidney Ellis

Opposite page: Governor Gretchen Whitmer reads a proclamation from the State of Michigan in recognition of the organization's 100th anniversary.
Photo by Aaron Cantrell

"Today's needs are much different than yesterday's."

A New Millennium

2000

Douglass staff exposed students to new and exciting places such as Greenfield Village in Dearborn, Michigan, and Brookfield Zoo. (Thehenryford.org)

Students who had never stepped foot outside of the city took part in Douglass-sponsored trips to places such as Greenfield Village in Dearborn, Michigan, and the Brookfield Zoo and museums in Chicago. Director Michael Williams provided the support to O'Neal Ollie to run the recreation programs to help students find their way in life. At the same time, Williams, the director, worked to keep all aspects of the organization running with support and approval from the board of directors.

Funds for the organization came from diverse streams. The community room provided adequate space for families and companies to rent for events and dance parties. The Kalamazoo Public Library leased space to house its Alma Powell branch, formerly located on North Burdick in the former Van Avery Drugstore. Federal and state funds for youth, mental health, legal aid, and job training programs were coupled with grants from local foundations and donors. The United Way also continued to provide substantial funding for operations, just as it had from the inception of the Douglass in the 1920s when they were known as Community Chest.

The resources the Douglass provided to the community made it indispensable. Although the local recreation centers opened their doors without prejudice, African Americans felt a sense of comfort as they sought services in a community with those who lived and understood their hopes and dreams. In addition, the counseling services had continued to expand to include more mental health, legal, and employment training.

By 2000, Williams had worked as director for thirteen years, but his connection with the organization went back decades. When Lee Roy Pettiford led the Douglass (1947-1962), Williams was a young boy. While he never remembers youth having contact with Pettiford, it was John Caldwell, Boys' director, who played a great role in his life.

Caldwell encouraged the boys to be their best, whether on the basketball court or in life. Williams remembers listening to boxing fights on the radio at the Ransom Street Douglass before many homes had television sets.

The foundation provided by the Douglass in sports and education led Williams to graduate from Kalamazoo Central and go on to play basketball at Ferris State University. While he didn't earn a degree from Ferris, he returned to Kalamazoo to attend Kalamazoo Valley Community College. There he won a Ford Foundation scholarship to Western Michigan University, earning bachelor's and master's degrees with concentrations in sociology, education, and social work.

His education and careers with KVCC and the State of Michigan made him a choice candidate for director of the Douglass. Williams' goal was to provide programming and activities that would benefit all of Kalamazoo, not just the city's Northside, particularly in the areas of mental health.

"(Mental health counseling) was one thing we were very proud of," Williams said. "From 1997-2005 we earned accreditation to do additional things in counseling. I was proud of the work that they did. I believe the reason we were successful was because we had minorities who worked on the staff; an Hispanic female director and other staff our clients could identify with. That went a long way in helping people with their mental health."

Williams said the challenge of billing for mental health services often led to a financial combat. Counselors needed to be meticulous in using the exact service number for each client based on their needs. If those numbers were wrong in any way, the payment request would be denied. Any incorrect numbering or hint of inconsistencies were forwarded to Williams as the director. If funds were not reimbursed, that left the organization holding the bag, a bag already stretched beyond its limits.

"My board did not seem to understand that other mental health agencies also complained about reimbursement issues. I tried to communicate that to my board, but they didn't seem to understand," Williams said.

The Douglass was in a financial crisis. In 2006, after almost nineteen years as director of the Douglass (longer than any other director in its history) Williams' role came to an end.

90-Year Celebration

After Williams' service to the organization, Valerie Cunningham was hired as interim director. However, before the year was out, Tim Terrentine took the helm. The 28-year-old leader had charisma and experience with youth and programming. He was a graduate of Kalamazoo Central and had earned bachelor's and master's degrees in the Arts from Western Michigan University. His three years as director of the "Proud 2 Be Me" program under Derek Jeter's Turn2 Foundation had made him a community leader in the area of youth advocacy.

By this time, Terrentine helped lead a youth-focused vision that "all Kalamazoo youth, especially youth living in the north and east side neighborhoods will have intellectual, physical and emotional support they need to achieve their full potential."

In addition to the Alma Powell Library, the Boys and Girls Club, City of Kalamazoo Safe Summer Playground, and Turn2 Foundation "Proud 2 Be Me" after-school program all leased space from the Center. Other programs housed in the Douglass included the Institute for New Leadership (Arcus Foundation) and ERACCE (Eliminating Racism and Claiming/Celebrating Equality).

The State of Michigan Department of Human Services contracted the organization's Family Advocate Program. The program provided support for families referred by Children's Protective Services who had been investigated for abuse. The Frederick Douglass Recovery Center also was a contracted program through Kalamazoo County Mental Health and Substance Abuse Services.

The Youth and Adult Services, all under the direction of O'Neal Ollie, included the Northside Rocket Football, Youth Basketball League, Developmental Basketball League, after-school tutoring services, adult co-ed volleyball, and the Donald Jackson Home Rehabilitation Services.

Under Terrentine's leadership, the Douglass was regaining some stability as well as acclaim as a premier community organization that served nearly 1,000 people each day. The doors were open from 7:30 a.m. to 2 a.m. with the conclusion of the Midnight Basketball games. The pinnacle moment for Terrentine was the 90-year celebration of the Douglass. Hundreds of dignitaries crowded into WMU's Bernhard Center to celebrate the Douglass' past and future potential. Former WMU President Dr. Elson Floyd served as keynote speaker during the February 20, 2010, event.

Tim Terrentine served as director of the Douglass Community Association during its 90-year celebration. Photo by Sean Hollins.

In the anniversary booklet for the event, Terrentine said of his work at the organization:

> *As we approached this milestone, I ponder on the meaning of our collective work in Kalamazoo. It is fitting that we were founded in honor of the abolitionist Frederick Augustus Washington Bailey a.k.a. Frederick Douglass. His work to free this nation of the sinful blot of slavery allows me the freedom I enjoy today. Contrary to the rhetoic of this "post-racial" discussion; WE must remain involved in the work of abolishing slavery. Not the slavery that is steeped in cotton, but the slavery of the mind. Frederick Douglass submitted that "once you learn to read; you will forever be free."*
>
> *In light of the Kalamazoo Promise and the ever-widening gulf of disparity in major quality of life areas for the most vulnerable populations, we are called to an aggressive abolitionists movement that situates literacy and education as our tools of dismantling the ignorance and despair that are too often the norm for the disenfranchised.*
>
> *I call on all of us to join the movement. This is a movement to emancipate the generations to come through collectively signing a new emancipation proclamation that will not, cannot wait for another time in history. This is our time! This is the place! We can free the children! We need only find the soul of the abolitionist.*

OUR VIEW

Douglass Association still doing important work

KG 2-14-10

For 90 years now, the Frederick Douglass Community Association has been providing opportunities for many people, but especially for young African-Americans living in the neighborhoods of north and east Kalamazoo.

Many people know, of course, that the association, which has its headquarters at 1000 W. Paterson St., was named for 19th century human rights pioneer Frederick Douglass, a former slave. The association, whose history goes back to July of 1919, was formed to provide black soldiers returning from World War I some of the same social opportunities afforded white soldiers.

Over the years, the association has been involved in social services, recreational programs, the civil rights movement, education and much more.

Today, the association works to provide opportunities in education, health, recreation and leadership, according to Tim Terrentine, the association's director. Terrentine and his staff work hard to encourage, teach, mentor and coach a large number of our young people, but Terrentine also is quick to point out that he and many others stand on the shoulders of a long line of dedicated people who have sought to improve the lives of youths in our city — and the city itself.

On Saturday, the association will celebrate its nine decades of service with a banquet featuring a keynote address by former Western Michigan University President Elson Floyd, who now is president of Washington State University.

Terrentine and former Executive Director Moses Walker, who spoke with editors and reporters at the Kalamazoo Gazette this past week about the association's history, are particularly proud of the fact that Floyd agreed to speak at the event. Floyd, of course, was WMU's first African-American president, but in the minds of Terrentine, Walker and others, he represents the kind of realized opportunity for young people that the association has in mind.

Education is cure for ignorance

Education, you see, is key to opportunity for a wide range of people. Terrentine described it this way: At the start, the association was about the work of an abolitionist, Douglass. Today, it's about freeing kids from the slavery of ignorance.

"We're going to save our kids Elson Floyd-style," he said.

The Kalamazoo Gazette joins with the rest of the community in congratulating the Douglass Community Association for 90 years of service to our young people and our city.

But the "association" is really the people — black, white and all — who dedicate themselves to lifting up the young, creating an environment of hope and possibility and providing the leadership young people need. So credit really goes to all the people — past and present — who do those things.

Because when they do them, they create a powerful product: opportunity.

Terrentine had grown with the Douglass. What he learned and the connections he made along the way propelled him into new territories. The Douglass had been a great stepping stone. However, he left to join the economic development organization Southwest Michigan First. He worked for the Chamber of Commerce program as executive vice president where he designed, developed, and facilitated more than fifteen regional leadership development programs, securing more than $100,000 in annual program sponsors.

After Terrentine, James Greene, a retired executive with Pharmacia and Upjohn, stepped in to serve as interim director. During his time of service from 2010-2013, financial instability—not unique to the organization over the decades—threatened the organization's future. Cuts had to be made. One of those was the Youth and Adult Services program that provided everything from Northside Rocket football to youth employment programs. More devastating, O'Neal Ollie, who had mentored hundreds of youth at the center for 27 years, was let go.

The More Things Change...

The financial problems of the Douglass had gone to a new low. When interim director James Greene moved out of his position, Moses Walker felt he had the right person to get the organization back on track.

Walker not only grew up at the Douglass as a preschooler, he served as its director from 1968-1978. He knew the loss of the Center would be devastating for the entire community. He went into rescue mode and called on his mentee to help. That friend was Sherry Thomas-Cloud. She had recently retired from the Department of Human Services and was teaching at Western Michigan University where years earlier she had earned her bachelor's and master's in social work.

At first she was hesitant to take on the job for fear of possibly being the one who would have to forever close its doors. When she toured the Center, she saw the students in the library. She saw herself in them. Toney Patterson, the head custodian and mentor to the kids, said the Douglass needed her. She decided to do her best to save it.

When she took the job, things were worse than she or the board knew. She inherited the issue of a boiler that had been broken so long that the gym had not been used in years. Buckets were placed in the hallways to catch water from the leaky roof. Creditors and contractors perched outside the director's office awaiting news of arrangements for long overdue payments. Her skeleton crew consisted of fewer than five people who were stretched thin, and she learned their health insurance had lapsed. However, her biggest challenge was to come three months after her arrival.

In 2013, the *Kalamazoo Gazette* began to publish news of the organization's financial woes due to the discontinuing of funds by the United Way of the Battle Creek and Kalamazoo Region. The United Way, formerly a Community Chest community funder, began its support of the Douglass in the 1920s. History had shown that, periodically, funds had ceased or had been on hold from the United Way due to financial and/or program inconsistencies the fiduciary felt did not meet their guidelines.

United Way 'deeply saddened' to drop funding for Douglass Community Association

BY ERIN GIGNAC
EGIGNAC@MLIVE.COM
KG 7-25-2013

KALAMAZOO — The United Way of the Battle Creek and Kalamazoo Region announced Wednesday it has discontinued funding for the Douglass Community Association, a 94-year-old organization that serves Kalamazoo's Northside Neighborhood.

The funding cut ends a partnership between Douglass and United Way that started in 1944.

"Regrettably, the situation has reached a point at which United Way believes that it cannot, in good conscience and good stewardship, continue to provide funding to the Douglass Community Association," Michael Larson, president and CEO of the United Way of the Battle Creek and Kalamazoo Region, said in a release.

The financial problems at Douglass have been building for several years, resulting in a "critical budget shortfall," Larson said. The United Way has offered guidance and funding throughout the financial difficulties in hopes the situation would improve.

The front entrance of the Douglass Community Association, at 1000 W. Paterson St. in Kalamazoo, is shown in this file photo.

"Unfortunately, the financial challenges at DCA have continued to mount," the release said.

James Liggins, Douglass Community Association board chairman, SEE DOUGLASS, A10

Children play in the Douglass Community Center on Thursday in Kalamazoo. The center lost a major funder and is struggling to stay open.

STEPH ANDERSON CHAMBERS | MLIVE.COM

The Douglass Community Center offers its own programs as well as a place for other organizations to operate.

Michael Larson, then president and CEO of the United Way, was quoted in a July 25, 2013, *Kalamazoo Gazette* article:

"Regrettably, the situation has reached a point at which United Way believes that it cannot, in good conscience and good stewardship, continue to provide funding to the Douglass Community Association."

While Larson said they "offered guidance and funding throughout the financial difficulties," the problem had become too massive to rectify. Financial reports provided to the United Way had sent "red flags" to the funders for years. In 2011, 53 people were employed by the organization. One of them was fired that year for embezzling $15,000 that was later replaced through an insurance claim. But the problem

Articles from the *Kalamazoo Gazette* (Kalamazoo Public Library).
Right: Powell Library children's program in Douglass Community Association.
Photo by Aaron Cantrell.

had been brewing for years. James Liggins, the Douglass board chair, replied (in the same 2013 article) that, "If we can't replace this funding and deal with financial issues, we very well may have to close."

The United Way was not the only funder who decreased or declined any funding. The Douglass' $1.1 million budget would lack more than $300,000 requested from a city block grant for youth programs. The Kalamazoo Community Foundation had provided more than $250,000 in grants from 2010-2011 and had now begun to close their purse strings to the Center as well.

While Thomas-Cloud had faith, she needed the board's full support to move forward. She called for a vote. Should they do everything in their power to save the community legacy or close its doors? The vote to close had to be unanimous.

As the vote moved forward, only two board members voted to keep the doors open. They wanted to fight for the place where children participated in the summer feeding program, Rocket football, the mental

health clinic, and the Powell branch library, among other services the Center housed. James Liggins, Jr., a local attorney, and Raymond Ryan, a supervisor with Consumers Energy, were both Kalamazoo natives who grew up benefiting from the programs and mentors. Their two "yes" votes provided Thomas-Cloud the validation she needed to give it her all.

Regaining Momentum

Ryan had grown up on Cobb Street, just a block from the Douglass. While in middle school, he frequented the new Center for its sports and the peace of the library where he could do his school work. It was the late '80s, and he saw how crime and drug activity stimulated by the crack cocaine epidemic worked to cripple his neighborhood. Some of his childhood friends were either selling or using drugs. He wanted no part of either.

As he grew older, he played in the Midnight Basketball program where pre-game talks were mandatory. The talks were initiated to motivate and educate youth on future choices. African American men who were part of the 100 Black Men organization had such professions as college professor, doctor, lawyer, and police officer, and spoke to the players. Topics from domestic violence to corporate etiquette were discussed in terms and with a passion the young men understood. For Ryan, it gave him mentors to look up to outside of sports and the music industry.

When he graduated from Kalamazoo Central in 1989 he immediately had employment through the Douglass internship program. The partnership with Portage Paper Company allowed upstanding young men from the basketball program to learn a trade or work in a field of interest. Ryan had an interest in electrical engineering and worked with the

Mt. Zion Baptist Church led fundraising and clean up projects in an effort to save the Douglass from closure due to lack of funds. Photo by Sean Hollins.

electrician department at the paper manufacturer while at the same time attending ITT Technical Institute. Although the company later folded, it provided Ryan the work experience he needed to eventually become Electric Field Leader for Consumers Energy.

The Douglass was the first board Ryan ever served on, and he had skin in the game. He and Liggins suggested churches be notified and brought on as leaders in the fight. Others such as Kalamazoo City Commissioner Stephanie Moore agreed to spread the word. Those of all ages throughout the entire community were asked to participate in clean up and painting efforts to refresh a once-prized jewel of the north side.

Thomas-Cloud had to find a way to "bridge the gap" for the nearly $270,000 the United Way discontinued as a funding stream. She went knocking on the doors of the churches, particularly those on the city's Northside.

Dr. Addis Moore, senior pastor of Mt. Zion Baptist Church, led the charge to raise $100,000 in thirty days in addition to a challenge to his church through a "Saving a Legacy" campaign. He encouraged 2,000 people to give at least $50 each. Dr. Michael T. Scott, Sr., senior pastor of Galilee Baptist Church, where Raymond Ryan was a deacon, hosted a Gospel Benefit Concert as letter-writing campaigns and meetings with donors ramped up. An "All Hands on Deck" clean-up day brought in hundreds of community residents who helped do everything from paint to cut shrubs.

Professional electricians and others provided more than $86,000 in services and in-kind donations.

Thomas-Cloud could not imagine what the Northside community would look like if the Douglass were missing. She had to let the community see that as well. Along with the fundraising, she secured a new advisory board that set efforts in place for transparency in accounting, professional oversight, a strategic plan, and new board members. It was the hardest work she had ever done.

In the end, in August of 2013, $101,469.38 was raised in the thirty days. The funds would hold over the organization for nearly four months of operating expenses. Thomas-Cloud credited the community, but more than that, she credited Ryan.

"It was Raymond who would not go out without a fight. He said, 'we should at least take a swing at it,' and we did," Thomas-Cloud said.

The victory would be bittersweet for Ryan. While he and Liggins provided the votes to move forward to save the Douglass, negotiations to remove past board members also were part of the new restructuring. However, his stand for the organization was his opportunity to do for the next generation what had been done for him.

As Thomas-Cloud worked to pay off old debts and move the organization forward, their fundraising totaled more than $500,000 by May of 2014. By July, the W.K. Kellogg Foundation awarded them a grant for nearly $300,000 for operations. The organization celebrated its 95th anniversary with an event at the Union on the downtown Mall. A silent auction of items donated from athletes who got their start at the Douglass helped raise funds for programming and operations. Items from football standouts T.J. Duckett and Greg Jennings went toward the cause.

Moving On

Thomas-Cloud helped get the organization back on track. She did not accept payment from the organization in 2016 as the new board reported a clean audit, more new donors, and a facility that was, once again, fully utilized. A strategic plan had led to a new vision: That all Kalamazoo youth, adults and families have the intellectual, physical and emotional support needed to achieve full potential.

It was now time for Thomas-Cloud to move on. The three years at the Douglass had been rewarding, but her job to save it was complete. She moved on to serve as chief executive director of Family & Children's Services after helping raise nearly $3 million for the Douglass.

In 2016, Cheree Thomas came on as director for two years to help move the revised efforts forward. During the 1980s and '90s the building bustled with services and recreation. She worked to regain that momentum as she solidified partnerships with current tenants such as the Helen Fox Music School, Kalamazoo Loaves and Fishes, Rootead Birthing Justice and Body Awareness, Momentum job and life skills training,

and Michigan Works! New and revised programs were scheduled with focuses on babies, preschoolers, teen girls and boys, fathers, and food distribution.

Then, in 2018, Sidney Ellis was hired to take on the job as executive director over the now seven staff members. He had formerly served as director of the Black Arts and Cultural Center, Kalamazoo Colleagues International, and as director of Mission Advancement of the Y.M.C.A. of Greater Kalamazoo. Ellis earned a bachelor's degree and MBA from Spring Arbor University.

Ellis brought his background in the arts and as a collaborator to the Douglass. He hit the ground running in January of 2019 when winter weather struck the nation with temperatures as low as 45 degrees below zero. The city's homeless were at risk of severe frostbite and even death,

Left: Thomas-Cloud holds the celebratory check as the community celebrates fundraising success. Photo by Sean Hollins.
Above: Kalamazoo Public Safety contributes time to youth at the Douglass Community Center. Photo by Aaron Cantrell.

and Ellis collaborated with the City of Kalamazoo to open the doors of the Douglass as a warming and feeding site. The Red Cross brought in cots and other agencies served hot meals.

After years of planning, a credit union was now on site for families in the community who sought a small yet convenient banking option. A branch of the local Community Promise Federal Credit Union was opened in the Douglass in 2019. However, this would not be the first time the organization attempted a credit union. In 1967 the organization opened a credit union in its Ransom Street building.

The Helen Fox Gospel Music Center and Rootead Enrichment Center are among community organizations housed in the Douglass Community Association. Photos provided by the Douglass Community Center.

Celebrating 100

Ellis' leadership coincided with the 100th year of the organization's founding. What started in 1919 as a place to provide entertainment for African American soldiers stationed at Fort Custer in nearby Battle Creek had diversified. Its mission now was to "create a culture of equality and inclusion that transforms the lives of Northside residents and beyond through effective, efficient, and quality opportunities."

The 2019 year of festivities kicked off with a press conference that included such dignitaries as Governor Gretchen Whitmer who toured the facility. An open house during Black History Month provided Ellis the opportunity to highlight the building partners and invite the community to family gatherings, a breakfast, and 100th anniversary gala. Tickets for the event were sold at $100 each in honor of the number of years the organization had served the community.

The 100th Anniversary Celebration was a star-studded event. From left, journalist Ed Gordon, Sidney Ellis, and Fenorris Pearson. Photo contributed by the Douglass Community Association.

In preparation for the event, Ellis hired Van Burch, a local videographer, to interview former directors, employees, and participants whose lives were impacted by the Douglass. He interviewed Juanita Goodwin and John Caldwell who had worked as youth directors at the Ransom Street center in the 1950s before becoming teachers in the Kalamazoo Public Schools.

Burch also captured on video an interview with Renaford Owens, Sr., who shared how his fondest memories were of his participation on the Douglass basketball team. During a time when many Y.M.C.A.s did not welcome African Americans in their recreation programs, Douglass filled the void. Owens and other players often had their first trips out of the city when they traveled to compete with other segregated

Top from left: Gus Calbert, long-time Douglass coach and mentor; 2019 Douglass Board members celebrate at a 100th anniversary event; Moses Walker and Buddy Hannah at Douglass fundraising event; Douglass tenants pose with new building signs. Photos by Aaron Cantrell.

centers like Douglass from Battle Creek to South Bend, Indiana. His wife, Vera, became the office manager at the Douglass years later.

Moses Walker also was on the interview list. He had led the organization from 1968 to 1978 through a transition from a recreation center to one that provided employment training and mental health counseling. He also was instrumental in forming the Family Health Center during his tenure before leaving to work for Borgess Hospital and later serving as a city commissioner. Walker shared his memories of being in preschool at the Douglass and of the organization's constant struggle to maintain financial stability.

Ida (Ollie) Buchanan's father owned Ollie's Barber Shop on North Burdick (later owned by Alex Walker). He was born in Memphis, Tennessee, and came to Battle Creek as a soldier at Fort Custer during World War II. He moved his family to Kalamazoo in 1955, where his children took part in Douglass activities. Young Ida remembers it being a place where she could play shuffleboard, cards, or ping pong with others in the lower level recreation room. She smiled as she recalled the snack bar and parties thrown in the gym.

A Salute to Legacy

On Saturday, September 28th, 2019, hundreds of dignitaries, community leaders, donors, and supporters participated in the gala affair to celebrate history. Ellis secured nationally-known journalist Ed Gordon to present the keynote address. One of the products of the Douglass' Midnight Basketball program, Fenorris Pearson, shared his reflections of how the mentors and scholarships provided by the Douglass were instrumental in his success as an author and business leader in a Fortune 500 company.

Ellis presented a surprise recognition to Toney Patterson, a man whose roots as a student athlete, coach, and employee of the Douglass inspired two generations of youth. Throughout the years, Patterson had shown extraordinary acts of kindness that included everything from hosting an impromptu birthday party for a girl who said she had never had a party, to providing lunch to kids who used the library as a safe haven.

Above: Douglass program alumnus and current employee Toney Patterson poses with Gov. Gretchen Whitmer after the presentation of a proclamation from the State that celebrated the 100th Anniversary of the Douglass Community Association. Opposite page: Local NAACP director Wendy Fields at 100th anniversary event. Photo contributed by the Douglass Community Association.

In his celebration message to the community, Ellis shared how the focus of the Douglass continuously evolved based on what the community needed most at that time. The staff has always worked to embrace everyone, from African American soldiers in need of a safe place to socialize to mothers needing to secure free diapers for their babies.

He wrote: *"Today's needs are much different than yesterday's. As the community's needs change, we plan to continue to adjust to accommodate those needs."*

AFTERWORD

By Sonya Hollins

When an executive director takes the helm of an organization a momentous challenge awaits. Many are in the lineage of others tasked to bring stability to an organization on the brink of a financial crisis. Other directors may be on a mission to create vision and partnerships. But what does it take to lead an organization into the future? That is what Sidney Ellis was called to do as he took the helm of the Douglass Community Association in 2018, on the verge of its 100th anniversary. That is where I come in.

Soon after his appointment, he realized that moving forward included a visit to the past. He asked if I would be up for the challenge to write the first historical chronicle of what is affectionately called The Douglass. As a native of Kalamazoo, I was honored. I would use my passion for local history and experience as a journalist to weave old news clippings and documents into a comprehensive journey. My husband, Sean, would use his graphic design magic to combine words and images to celebrate a community's legacy.

Little did Ellis know, I had a desire to share the story of the Douglass in my own way before he dialed my number. Just a few months prior to his call, I had asked a friend and local realtor, Twala Lockett, to take me into the "old" Douglass at 231 Ransom Street. I passed the building each day and was drawn to its boarded windows and unkempt lawn. I saw the character in the bricks of the corner property that was listed for sale at $50,000. What could I do to revive this building and celebrate its history? There were endless possibilities.

When Twala, Sean, and I arrived at the location on a bright fall day, she unlocked the heavy metal door and pushed it open. Immediately, she gave Sean the flashlight to lead the way through the building where only beams of sun shone through cracks of the boarded windows. We felt like spies in a black-and-white mystery thriller as we were met with cool stale air, crumbling walls, and hints of the birds and rodents who took up residency in its walls and ceilings.

We tipped through the lower level where a squatter's blanket was pushed into a corner. Twala shared how, at one point, the Merry Makers organization planned to revive the building into a place for community events. Now, dusty china and silverware spilled onto the floor out of weakened cardboard boxes that awaited a dream which never came true. In spite of its appearance, the building's foundation was solid. The massive community gymnasium contained an auditorium stage and balcony. I recalled images of handsome Colored soldiers in their World War II uniforms who danced on those floors with pretty brown women who smiled at the camera. The horns and drums of local musicians dressed in crisp white suits once played Big Band hits in the very spot I stood. Now, a leaky roof dripped onto abandoned metal chairs where decades earlier leaders discussed ways to bring jobs and opportunities to the Black community.

My vision of what the old Douglass could become began to fade like an overexposed film. I was overwhelmed by the monumental feat of upgrades to the electrical and plumbing systems and removal of lead paint and possible asbestos. The estimated cost of my dream doubled with every turn. The manpower needed to bring everything up to code was beyond my resources. My heart sank.

When Ellis called to propose the history book project I thought, *This can be my way to bring life to this history.* As a journalist, I knew I needed people to help tell the story; people who lived through the history or had access to the information. Dorothy Young, former principal of Hillside Junior High, was my principal when I attended the school. She was well connected in the community and would be a great start. She loaned me an event program booklet and said, "This should give you some ideas on who to talk to." She had treasured the booklet since 1984, the day of the grand opening of the "new" Douglass Community Center at 1000 W. Paterson Street. That booklet set me on a path to tell the story.

In 1919 racial tension brewed in America. World War I had ended months earlier and soldiers who fought, Black and White, returned home. Black migrants from the South had filled manual labor jobs once reserved for White men. Whites felt Blacks had taken their jobs. Then, the match was struck. The pot of racial tension came to a roaring boil in the heat of the summer. A young Black Chicago boy floated too closely to the "Whites Only" beach area on Lake Michigan. He was stoned and drowned by Whites who abhorred the audacity of a Black person who dared pollute their space with his presence. Police refused to arrest the culprits. Blacks were outraged. That anger led to riots that spilled over into other major cities throughout the country. The bloodshed and violence from those riots precipitated what would be called Red Summer.

Black men in Kalamazoo heard the news. The Ku Klux Klan had a chapter in the city and they were known to boldly march in parades through town wearing white sheets to shield their identities. During that same time, thousands of soldiers stationed at nearby Camp Custer in Battle Creek came to Kalamazoo for recreation during weekend furloughs. The Black soldiers, however, did not have a Soldiers Club to attend, as did their White counterparts. This left hundreds of men in a town without a place to have a drink or play a game of pool. The racial climate coupled with Black men who roamed downtown in uniform was a disaster waiting to happen. Forrest Hill and his friends decided to create a safe place for these soldiers to prevent riots in their own community.

After discussions and partnerships with local White leaders, Hill and his friends helped found the Frederick Douglass Center. Their first home was on the second floor of a former Turn Verein Hall (a German gymnasium) located on North Burdick Street in Kalamazoo's downtown. That hall not only provided a place of recreation and community support for soldiers, but it also gave a spacious gathering place for women and children to read and take part in activities not granted at the local Y.M.C.A. Directors helped take the vision further and eventually purchased land to build their own organization.

In February 1941, excitement was in the air as hundreds came out for the grand opening of the Douglass Community Center at 231 Ransom Street. I can only imagine what youth felt as they ran along the shiny floor of the new gymnasium, or the ideas women had for auxiliary group affairs and fancy dances. City mayors and dignitaries celebrated alongside soldiers and youth. This beautifully crafted two-story building included a recreation center in the basement with ping pong and pool tables. There was a cozy library filled with books by African American poets and novelists. Tiny chairs and tables awaited little ones in a preschool room, and offices included professional filing cabinets and typewriters. Never before had African Americans in Kalamazoo built such a grand facility from the ground up. They had raised nearly $150,000 to create this safe haven for the community.

As I thumbed through yellowed newspaper clippings, I discovered 100 years of trials and triumphs of the Frederick Douglass Community Center (later Association replaced Center). I was on a rollercoaster ride where funders dangled carrots of resources before their board members if programs were adjusted to their expectations only to remove the funding at their will. I read of recreation counselors like Juanita Goodwin and John Caldwell who partnered with parents as mentors who instilled pride and self-respect in the children who came to the Douglass. I read how a community home painting program gave young men their first jobs, and how basketball programs were less about the sport and more about the game of life.

After months of interviews and research, my heartache for the 231 Ransom Street building subsided. While the building had been neglected, the mission had not. Forrest Hill and his friends had gathered in his living room in 1919 to find out how they could make a difference in their community. A century later, the community joined to rescue the organization on the brink of closure. The Douglass was more than a building. As of the publishing of this book, the abandoned Douglass on 231 Ransom Street sits in desolate silence as luxury apartments are built up around it. The door that once welcomed Head Start students or dads who sought employment services is bolted shut. But, through the new Douglass and directors who each brought their unique talents, the legacy continues.

The completion of this book, like the end of our old Douglass tour, was bittersweet. As the research concluded and the design was finalized, I thought back on the day of the tour nearly two years prior. When my husband and I walked through its people-deprived halls with the realtor, we could only imagine what things had been like in the building's infancy. As we prepared to leave the ghosts of the past behind and rejoin the world, I noticed a mosaic backsplash image on the wall of a water fountain. I snapped a photo of it with my phone, in hopes of possibly having it relocated to Pretty Lake Camp, where, at the time, I was board president.

The image was designed and dedicated to Edward Desenberg, the founder of Pretty Lake Camp. He was one of the prominent White men Forrest Hill approached to help form the original Douglass. Desenberg died in 1940, just weeks before the ground breaking of the Ransom Street building. However, the scripture on that fountain is a testament to Desenberg, the men who saw the vision to reality, and the spirit of all whose hearts were dedicated to a community institution.

"He who is gracious to the needy honoreths God." *Proverbs 14:31 (NIV)*

The Douglass is more than a building. The Douglass is a ministry, a safe haven, and an opportunity to give back to the community what it needs to move forward into the future.

S.H.

This fountain was located in the Ransom Street Douglass and was dedicated to Edward Desenberg, the founder of Pretty Lake Camp and one of the prominent local leaders who saw the significance of a place where children and adults could enjoy recreation.
Photo by
Sonya Bernard-Hollins.

ACKNOWLEDGMENTS

There is no way this book would have been possible without the many people who gave their time to bring 100 years of history to life. But, most importantly, I thank God, who knew more than 100 years ago that the people connected to the Douglass' story—many who would never know the others—would all come together a century later through this project.

Sidney Ellis, executive director of the Douglass Community Association, believed in Sean and me to bring 100 years of documents, photos, missing, and newly discovered information together. Those who know me know that I LOVE history! This was truly a challenge I was more than ready to take on.

My husband Sean Hollins of Fortitude Graphic Design and Printing brought on his creativity to the words. He took the photos and wove them into 100 years of digital storytelling that readers can appreciate before they even read a word.

Thanks to Dorothy Young for opening the door to the beginnings of the Douglass. To Matt Smith of Kalamazoo Public Library's Local History Room, whose eager assistance was invaluable! When he learned of my work on this project, he pulled out any document, article, or book he could find to help answer stories. When I could not find any photos of the first Douglass location on North Burdick, he dove into the local phone directories of decades past to locate the address of the office. In addition, once that was discovered, the location above Lakey's Paint Store was found to be the first home of the community center. To us, it was a goldmine-type find.

The historic records of the Douglass by the *Kalamazoo Gazette, Kalamazoo News, and Focus* newspapers proved the importance of positive and not-so-flattering objective media coverage of all communities. Tom Vance of the Kalamazoo Community Foundation shared minutes from meetings with local leaders as they were approached to support a future Douglass Community Center for Black soldiers.

Those who lived the history were the most valuable. Interviews at the Douglass and past interviews archived at the Kalamazoo Valley Museum provided the glue that connected news articles and old photos together. Those such as Juanita Goodwin and John Caldwell gave me the personal experience from them as youth workers. Their passion to provide quality athletic recreation to youth that led to self-esteem, teamwork, mentorship, and so much more, did more than they imagined.

Interviews with Moses Walker, a former director of the Douglass, shared how, even as a student at the Head Start in the Douglass, he had pride in attending class in a building his own father had helped build as a laborer hired by the Works Progress Administration. It was heartbreaking that both Walker and Goodwin passed away before the book was published.

To my children, Shamiel, Syann, and Sasha who learned how to use a scanner and microfilm to help catalog the dozens of news articles in the Douglass files at the Kalamazoo Public Library. They wondered why Google didn't have the information at their fingertips. They learned, there was life before Alexa…and they don't envy it one bit.

To Maggie Zahrai who worked to edit each chapter as I tapped away. Just as fast as I sent her the chapters, she returned them with valuable insight and questions. My desire to often assume certain events or actions was halted by her ability to make me answer things that were vague, or, for the things I could not answer or confirm, to just "leave it out." And, to my fellow scribe Jayda Craig, who reviewed the final drafts to provide valuable input and editing remarks.

There is no way I can name everyone who played some role in this project, but know you all are appreciated. None of this would be possible without the small and major roles you played to bring this history to life.

Thank you all!

S.H.

SELECTIVE
BIBLIOGRAPHY
&
INDEX

The Beginning

Walters, Barbara. "They Helped Fight Loneliness," *Kalamazoo Gazette,* September 25, 1987, pg. A1, A2.

Horton, James Oliver. *A History of African American People: The History, Traditions & Culture of African Americans,* Salamander Books, Ltd, 1995, New York, NY.

Csete, Josephine. *Emancipated Spirits: Portraits of Kalamazoo College Women,* June 1990, Kalamazoo, Michigan, Ihling Bros. Everard Co.

McKissack, Frederick. *Days of Jubilee: The End of Slavery in the United States,* Scholastic Press, New York, 2003.

History.com. "World War I," https://www.history.com/topics/world-war-i/world-war-i-history

Trace Christenson. "Fort Custer Reaches Century Mark," *Battle Creek Enquirer,* July 1, 2017. https://www.battlecreekenquirer.com/story/news/local/2017/07/01/fort-custer-reaches-century-mark/445820001/

Kalamazoo County Michigan Genealogy on the Web. "Interurbans." http://www.migenweb.org/kalamazoo/rail-roadsinterurbansp2.htm

Johnson, Pauline. "The Beginning: Douglass Community Association Through the Eyes of Pauline Johnson," 1984 Souvenir Program, Frederick Douglass Community Association, Kalamazoo, Michigan.

Mayer, Elizabeth. *Yes, There were Germans in Kalamazoo: A Short Study of the German Element and its Influence in Kalamazoo County, Michigan, 1830-1978,* Kalamazoo (Michigan) County Historical Society, 1979.

Smith, Sande. "Frederick Douglass," *Who's Who in African American History,* 1994, Brompton Books Corp., New York.

"Ex-Slave is Linked to Pre-Civil War Quakers," *The Enquirer And News,* November 8, 1959 Section 2, Page 1.

1920s

Community Chest of Kalamazoo Co., Inc.; "Please," annual funders report, 1928, page 31.

Community Chest of Kalamazoo Co., Inc.; "Kalamazoo Cares," 1926 annual report, page 7.

1906 Kalamazoo City and County Directory, Kalamazoo, Michigan.

1921 Kalamazoo City and County Directory, Kalamazoo, Michigan.

"Germanic Influence Felt Here." *Kalamazoo Gazette,*

"Gymnasium Instructor," *Kalamazoo Daily Telegraph,* August 5, 1885, pg. 3. Salem, Dorothy C. *African American Women: A Biographical Dictionary, Volume 2,* Garland Publishing, New York, 1993.

Case Western Reserve University Encyclopedia of Cleveland History. http://\www.case.edu/ech/articles/m/mitchell-l-pearl

Cunningham, Emil L. "Wilberforce University: The Early Years (1856-1900)," *The History of American Higher Education*, Pennsylvania State University, http://sites.psu.edu/wp-content/uploads/sites/12965/2011/06/Wilberforce-Research-Paper.pdf

"Former International Presidents," Alpha Kappa Alpha Sorority, Inc. https://aka1908.com/about/former-international-presidents

Attwell, Ernest T. "Recreation for Colored America," *The American City Magazine*, New York, New York, pgs. 161-166.

1930s

"What Welfare Federation Agencies Are Doing," *Kalamazoo Gazette*, October 31, 1930.

"E.W. Powell Will Arrive Tonight," *Kalamazoo Gazette*, July 30, 1934.

"Plan Reception for Douglass Director," *Kalamazoo Gazette*, July 31, 1934.

"U.S. Recreation Program to Open Here on Thursday," *Kalamazoo Gazette*, June 27, 1934.

"Douglass Center Activities Expand," *Kalamazoo Gazette*, January 1, 1935.

"Colored Boys Will go to Camp Monday," *Kalamazoo Gazette*, April 21, 1935.

"Kalamazoo Negro Center May Get $44,000 Building," *Kalamazoo Gazette*, June 2, 1935.

"Douglass Center Benefit Garden Party Draws Crowd," *Kalamazoo Gazette*, June 14, 1935.

"Douglass Center to Open its 18th Season on Oct. 1," *Kalamazoo Gazette*, September 27, 1936.

"Douglass Club to Have Musical Tea," *Kalamazoo Gazette*, November 8, 1936.

Powell, Alma. "Douglass Community Center," personal journal entry, 1938.

"Douglass Center Shows Increase," *Kalamazoo Gazette*, January 6, 1938.

"200 to Attend Douglass Camp," *Kalamazoo Gazette*, June 15, 1938.

"Douglass Center Picnic Thursday," *Kalamazoo Gazette*, July 30, 1938.

"Douglass Center Girls Plan Amateur Contest," *Kalamazoo Gazette*, July 7, 1938.

"Error Cancels Negro Center Project Here," *Kalamazoo Gazette*, August 6, 1938.

"Douglass Center Turns Over Deed," *Kalamazoo Gazette*, September 13, 1938.

"Douglass Center Program to Open," *Kalamazoo Gazette*, October 3, 1938.

"Propose $71,900 Douglass Center," *Kalamazoo Gazette*, November 1, 1938.

"Resume Drive for Douglass Center," *Kalamazoo Gazette*, November 3, 1938.

"Douglass Center Sets Camp Dates," *Kalamazoo Gazette*, May 31, 1939.

"Commission Acts to Give Douglass Center New Home," *Kalamazoo Gazette*, April 27, 1937.

"Raise $17,600 for Douglass Center Building," *Kalamazoo Gazette*, May 16, 1939.

"Douglass Center Building Assured," *Kalamazoo Gazette*, May 25, 1939.

1940s

"Douglass Center Activities Have Difficult Year," *Kalamazoo Gazette*, January 4, 1940.

"Douglass Group is After $6,000," *Kalamazoo Gazette*, January 18, 1940.

Powell, E.N. "A Dollar or More Drive," Douglass Community Center
        fundraising letter, January 20, 1940.

"Death Takes Pretty Lake Camp Founder," *Kalamazoo Gazette*, January 21, 1940.

"Douglass Center to Break Ground," *Kalamazoo Gazette*, February 15, 1940.

"Ground Broken for New Negro Center Project," *Kalamazoo Gazette*,
        February 18, 1940.

"Group Sponsors Camping Periods," *Kalamazoo Gazette*, June 2, 1940.

"Camp for Colored Boys Opens Aug. 11," *Kalamazoo Gazette*, August 4, 1940.

"Professional Football Game to Benefit Two Settlement Projects,"
        Kalamazoo Gazette, September 12, 1940.

"Meeting Social Responsibility in Kalamazoo," Community Chest of Kalamazoo
        County, Inc. annual giving report, October 1, 1940.

"Increases Aid for Douglass Center," *Kalamazoo Gazette*, November 22, 1940.

"Douglass Party to Honor Memory of Edward Desenberg," *Kalamazoo Gazette*,
        December 15, 1940.

"Douglass Center Will Occupy New Building Feb. 1," *Kalamazoo Gazette*,
        January 12, 1941.

"Dedication of New Douglass Center Today," *Kalamazoo Gazette*, February 16, 1941.

"New Douglass Center Opened at Ceremonies," *Kalamazoo Gazette*, February 17, 1941.

"Kindergarten to Open at Center," *Kalamazoo Gazette*, November 30, 1941.

"Seventeen Colored Children Enroll in Town Camp," *Kalamazoo Gazette*, June 6, 1942.

"Reception to Honor Douglass Center Chief," *Kalamazoo Gazette*, April 12, 1945.

"Douglass Center Marks Birthday," *Kalamazoo Gazette*, November 14, 1945.

"Douglass Center Adds Director," *Kalamazoo Gazette*, April 4, 1946.

"John D. Ridley Named Douglass Center Director," *Kalamazoo Gazette*, June 9, 1946.

"L.R. Pettiford Named Douglass Center Director," *Kalamazoo Gazette*,
        September 22, 1947.

"Douglass Center has New Worker," *Kalamazoo Gazette*, December 14, 1947.

"Open Douglass Stay-at Home Camp June 28," *Kalamazoo Gazette*, June 20, 1948.

"Douglass Center Plans Program on 29th Anniversary," *Kalamazoo Gazette*,
        November 19, 1948.

"Work Progress Administration," https://www.history.com

1950s

"Douglass Drive Opens Wednesday," *Kalamazoo Gazette*, May 7, 1950.

"Douglass Ends Record Drive," *Kalamazoo Gazette*, June 4, 1950.

"Douglass to Open Camping Roles Monday," *Kalamazoo Gazette*, June 11, 1950.

"Instal Staff at Douglass," *Kalamazoo Gazette*, June 13, 1950.

"Douglass Center Group Anticipates Banner Year," *Kalamazoo Gazette*, July 4, 1950.

"Stay-at-Home Camp Opening at Douglass," *Kalamazoo Gazette*, June 24, 1951.

"Douglass Community Center Carries on an Extensive and Varied Program,"
        Kalamazoo Gazette, September 19, 1951.

"Douglass Community Unit Aims at 'American Ideal,'" *Kalamazoo Gazette*,
      September 24, 1952.
"Douglass Youth Council Formed," *Kalamazoo Gazette*, September 25, 1952.
"Douglass Assn. Appoints Boys Work Director," *Kalamazoo Gazette*, March 3, 1956.
"Douglass Center Offers Program for All Ages," *Kalamazoo Gazette*, October 21, 1956.

1960s
Fifties Web - fiftiesweb.com/pop/inventions-60/"Heading North, He Donates Farm,"
Kalamazoo Gazette, April 24, 1960.
Rauch, Victor. "The Race Issue: Kalamazoo's School Desegregation Case Made History,"
      Museography, page 2.
Belsie,Laurent. "In Kalamazoo, Calm After the Storm: A Generation of School Desegre-
      gation has Eased Racial Tensions Between Blacks and Whites, Christian Science
      Monitor, February, 16, 1989.
"Van Avery Drugstore Protest Anniversary," *MuseOn*, Summer 2018.
"Douglass Purpose Changed," *Kalamazoo Gazette*, May 6, 1962.
"City May Take Over Douglass Recreation," *Kalamazoo Gazette*, November 6, 1962.
"Douglass Area Open as Gardens," *Kalamazoo Gazette*, April 14, 1963.
"Douglass Community's Acting Director Resigns," *Kalamazoo Gazette*, January 4, 1964.
"Executive Director Appointed by Douglass Community Center Board,"
      Kalamazoo Gazette, July 5, 1964.
"'Take Me as I Am' New Douglass Director Insists," *Kalamazoo Gazette*,
      October 11, 1964.
"Douglass Association Receives $200,000 Grant," *Kalamazoo Gazette*,
      November 20, 1964.
"Introduction of Douglass Head Planned," *Kalamazoo Gazette*, December 4, 1964.
"Douglass Results May Show in '65" *Kalamazoo Gazette*, January 26, 1965.
"Douglass Center Adds to its Staff," *Kalamazoo Gazette*, June 13, 1965.
"Douglass Director Resigns," *Kalamazoo Gazette*, May 30, 1965.
"New Director for Douglass Appointed," *Kalamazoo Gazette*, June 6, 1965.
"Departing Director of Douglass Cites Value of Social Planning," *Kalamazoo
      Gazette*, August 21, 1965.
"City's Douglass Center Signs New 'Quarterback,'" *Kalamazoo Gazette*,
      September 5, 1965.
"Douglass Plan to Enlarge Services Receives Backing," *Kalamazoo Gazette*,
      April 26, 1966.
"Wyatt Kirk President of Douglass," *Kalamazoo Gazette*, June 22, 1966.
"Credit Union First of its Kind in State," *Focus*, February, 1967, page 4.
"Douglass Purposes Reviewed," *Kalamazoo Gazette*, June 9, 1967.
"Intrefol Wins Federal Grant of $41,962," *Kalamazoo Gazette*, July 17, 1967.
"'Intrefol' Program at Douglass is Enlarged," *Kalamazoo Gazette*, August 5, 1967.
"Complain Directly to Douglass, Kirk Urges," *Kalamazoo Gazette*, May 23, 1968.

"Date Changed in 'Poor' Campaign," *Kalamazoo Gazette*, May 24, 1968.

"Moses Walker to Start Job at Douglass Center," *Kalamazoo Gazette*, June 9, 1968.

"Church Council Delays on Hiring Organizer," *Kalamazoo Gazette*, June 11, 1968.

"Local Residents Plan Trip to Mass Rally," *Kalamazoo Gazette*, June 13, 1968.

"Wade Urges Regular Savings in North Community Credit Union," *Focus*, April 1969, page 3.

"Caldwell is Douglass President," *Kalamazoo Gazette*, August 2, 1968.

"40 Applicants Sought for Local Job Openings," *Kalamazoo Gazette*, August 21, 1968.

"Douglass Director Defends Record, Supports Ed Morris' Appointment," *Kalamazoo Gazette*, August 26, 1968.

"Douglass Board Backs Director in Statement," *Kalamazoo Gazette*, August 26, 1968.

"James Horn to Leave for New Post," *Kalamazoo Gazette*, October 11, 1968.

"Aide Named Acting Head at Douglass," *Kalamazoo Gazette*, November 15, 1968.

"Douglass Center Staff Changes Announced," *Kalamazoo Gazette*, February 16, 1969.

"Douglass to Mark 50th Year," *Kalamazoo Gazette*, July 13, 1969.

"50 Years for Douglass Association," *Kalamazoo Gazette*, July 20, 1969.

"Eight Members Elected by DCA Board," *Kalamazoo Gazette*, August 1, 1969.

"Caldwell Reelected at Douglass," *Kalamazoo Gazette*, September 12, 1969.

"Cutback of Federal Funds Clouds Douglass Programs, *Kalamazoo Gazette*, September 22, 1969.

1970s

"Rolls Voted President of Douglass," *Kalamazoo Gazette*, (no date).

"'Free School' Concept Aired," *Kalamazoo Gazette*, September 9, 1970.

"DCA Unit Sets Annual Yule Party," *Kalamazoo Gazette*, December 13, 1970.

"Casual Labor Office Set Up at Douglass," *Kalamazoo Gazette*, September 19, 1971.

"From the Bottom Up," *Kalamazoo Gazette*, April 22, 1972.

"Douglass' Influence Countrywide," *Kalamazoo Gazette*, September 22, 1974.

"Rolls Again Heads Local Douglass Unit," *Kalamazoo Gazette*, June 24, 1971.

"Paterson Clinic Renamed Moses L. Walker Building," Family Health Center, October 29, 2017.

1980s

"Douglass Community Celebrates," *Kalamazoo News*, June 18, 1980.

"Meet the Staff," *Northside Communicator*, January 1983.

Board of Directors Message, Douglass Community Association Program Booklet, October 27, 1984.

"Headed for the Nationals," *Kalamazoo Gazette* (date unknown).

"Lone Wolf Still Active," *Kalamazoo News*, Feb. 24-March 1, 1984.

1990s

Douglass Community Association brochure, 1991.

"Resurrecting the old Douglass center," *Kalamazoo Gazette*, September 12, 1999.

"Center has played a pivital role," Kalamazoo Gazette, September 12, 1999.

"Douglass: 'Seminal Role' in Change," *Kalamazoo Gazette*, December 2, 1999.

2000s

"Douglass Association still doing important work," *Kalamazoo Gazette*, February 14, 2010.

"90th Anniversary Celebration," Douglass Community Association program booklet, February 20, 2010

"A Void that will not be filled" Douglass Community Center Could Close over Funding Problems," *Kalamazoo Gazette*, July 21, 2013.

"Douglass Community Association director leaving," *Kalamazoo Gazette*, April 16, 2010.

"United Way 'deeply saddened' to drop funding for Douglass Community Association," *Kalamazoo Gazette*, July 25, 2013.

"Fighting for its life: Douglass Community Association Battling to Keep Organization Alive in Face of Funding Deadline," *Kalamazoo Gazette*, August 4, 2013.

"Campaign underway to keep Douglass Community," *Kalamazoo Gazette*, August 17, 2013.

"Goal: $100,000 in 30 days: Campaign Seeks to Help Save Douglass Community Association," *Kalamazoo Gazette*, August 20, 2013.

"Douglass Association supporters 'stand their ground:' 94-year-old organization needs $100K in a month to stay open," August 21, 2013.

"Thirty-day fundraiser helps in Saving a Legacy," *Kalamazoo Gazette*, September 5, 2013.

"Money from Douglass Community Association fundraising campaign won't pay $107K tax bill," *Kalamazoo Gazette*, September 7, 2013.

"Hundreds work to preserve Douglass Community center," *Kalamazoo Gazette*, August 23, 2013.

"Douglass association gets grant: Kellogg Foundation gives organization $297K," *Kalamazoo Gazette*, July 11, 2014.

"Community association official: 'It's a long-term fix," *Kalamazoo Gazette*, May, 17, 2014.

"Almost from the ashes up," *Kalamazoo Gazette*, February 8, 2015.

"Douglass to mark 95th anniversary," *Kalamazoo Gazette*, February 3, 2015.

Community association official: 'It's a long-term fix," *Kalamazoo Gazette*, May, 17, 2014.

"Almost from the ashes up," *Kalamazoo Gazette*, February 8, 2015.

"Shaking the hand of the past and welcoming the hand of the future," Douglass Community Association 100th Anniversary program booklet, September 28, 2019.

Made in the USA
Monee, IL
29 July 2021